Presence Carriers

DAVID SHEARMAN

RIVER
PUBLISHING

River Publishing & Media Ltd
Barham Court
Teston
Maidstone
Kent
ME18 5BZ
United Kingdom

info@river-publishing.co.uk

ISBN 978-1-908393-06-7
Printed in the United Kingdom

Contents

Acknowledgements

To the leaders and many members of the Christian Centre family who have helped me on my journey and been patient with my many "learnings".

To the many leaders and friends who have encouraged me on life's journey.

To Jonathan Bugden for welcoming and encouraging my ideas.

To Tim Pettingale who has been with me in all my published book writing and who especially helped me re-shape this book and spur me on to a finish.

To my family whose love and support are priceless, especially Sarah whose industry on the manuscript was beyond the call of duty.

To my "Cinders" – Buttons will always love you...

And finally, to "....Jesus Christ our Lord, who is alive and reigns with you and the Holy Spirit, one God, world without end. Amen."

Part One

Introduction
– the Genesis

The genesis of this book has been a long time in development. After more than fifty years as a Christ-follower, my search for a deeper experience of the presence of God has intensified. This is not to say I despise what has gone before. I am grateful to God for a Pentecostal heritage with its commitment to "living in the Spirit", miracles and the power of prophecy.

I am grateful for years of experience in extemporaneous prayer with its inspirational component – an understanding that "our weapons are spiritual" and that there is a warfare dimension to prayer and living. I am grateful that I was taught that the Bible – the Holy Scriptures are God-breathed, living and active and to be believed, received, confessed and lived out. I am grateful that I grew up in a home where the presence of God was valued, with parents who were prayerful, active and sacrificial in applying their faith, and in a church where knowing the presence of God was desired more than any prepared programme.

I am grateful too for many godly examples, people who walked into and through my life as a "son of the manse". Very different people in a multitude of ways – breeding and background, training and temperament, education and eloquence; some funny and, yes, some fanatical. The descriptions could continue. All were, in their unique way, *presence carriers*. God knew them and they "knew" God. Each seemed to carry the presence, whether in the special or the ordinary events of life.

I will talk later about some of the challenges to my known spirituality that came from monks and mystics, people whose journey to knowing God had developed along different pathways to my own. Some of these experiences have been unsettling, even disturbing, challenging long held ideas, maybe even prejudices; but always, eventually, if applied well, hugely beneficial. However far back I go in my life, describing what the Psalmist expressed in the words, *"My soul thirsts for God, for the living God"* and *"When can I go and meet with God?"* I still won't come to the fundamental genesis of these writings. For however much I long to know God, it has been a long and dawning revelation, a breathtaking truth, that before I was born He knew me, created me in my mother's womb and longs with a deep passion to have an intimate relationship with me.

You and I are here on this earth because an uncreated, uncaused and unaccountable being we call God, even though He is complete in Himself, wants someone to love and share eternity with and that someone is you and me!

Poets and painters, prelates, prophets and philosophers have searched this deep water from the beginning of time. We are both helped and hindered by the content of their searching for we can be dazed and confused and find no focus in their many voices. When we lose the simple wonder of God's immeasurable love for us we will always be and live less than we were intended without knowing Him. However successful we may be in life, if we do not carry His presence in what the Bible calls *"the temple of the Holy Spirit"*, our bodies, then we will be unfulfilled.

I believe it was the great theologian Karl Barth who, when asked what was the most profound truth he had learned from his many years of mining the Scriptures, responded, "Jesus loves me, this I know, for the Bible tells me so."

I am immediately conscious that my readership is divided. Some enjoy a knowing relationship with God and consciously want to know Him more. Some don't know whether God is real or can be known. Others, disillusioned by life's unanswered "whys" and poor examples of Christians have turned away, even forgotten that God exists. Some don't think they are good enough to personally know God. Still others know a spiritual emptiness and an inner longing, but don't know for what.

Wherever you are on the spectrum of "knowing God" let me endeavour to assure you that the God I have come to know wants you to know Him. He is not playing hide and seek, but gives us the assurance that, *"You will seek me and find me when you seek me with all your heart"* (Jeremiah 29:13).

Let me state for the record that I am not writing as the "expert", the know-it-all. Rather, my writing describes some of my stumbling journey and my convictions and gratitude that the God who created everything and needs nothing, revealed Himself to me before I showed any inclination towards Him.

I would be honoured if you think it worthwhile to journey through this book with me. My prayer as I write and you read is that we will have "epiphanies", meetings, revelations, life-changing moments that will help each of us know that God is bigger than we ever imagined, nearer than we think, more wonderful than the grandest description of Him, and that He wants to dignify our lives with His presence.

Enjoy the journey.

David Shearman
Nottingham, April 2012

P.S. You may be impatient to engage with the implications of being a Presence Carrier. If so (prayerfully) consider reading Part 2 and return to the beginning later. The more patient among us will lay a foundation by reading part 1 first!

1
Lost in the Jungle

Whether we are aware of it on a daily basis or not, each of us is embarked on a pilgrimage through this life. We are all engaged in a process of discovering who we really are and what we were put on this earth to do. If you believe, as I do, that an ever-deepening experience of God's presence is a vital key to understanding both of these things, how is it that, despite this experience being a vibrant reality for many believers, still a great many are "lost" in various jungles?

Max Lucado tells the following story in his book *Travelling Light*:

Your friends convinced you it was time for a once-in-a-lifetime trip, and here you are. You paid the fare. You crossed the ocean. You hired the guide and joined the group. And you ventured where you had never ventured before – into the thick, strange world of the jungle.

Sound interesting? Let's take it a step farther. Imagine that you are in the jungle, lost and alone. You paused to lace your boot, and when you looked up, no one was near. You took a chance and went to the right; now you're wondering if the others went to the left. (Or did you go left and they go right?)

Whatever, you are alone. And you have been alone for, well, you don't know how long it has been. Your watch was attached to your pack, and your pack is on the shoulder of the nice guy from New Jersey who volunteered to hold it while you tied your boots. You didn't intend for him to walk off with it. But he did. And here you are, stuck in the middle of nowhere.

You have a problem. First, you were not made for this place. Drop you in the centre of avenues and buildings and you could sniff your way home. But here in sky-blocking foliage? Here in trail-hiding thickets? You are out of your element. You weren't made for this jungle. What's worse you aren't equipped. You have no machete. No knife. No matches. No flares. No food. You aren't equipped, but now you are trapped – and you haven't got a clue how to get out.

Sound like fun to you? Me either. Before moving on, let's pause and ask how you would feel. Given such circumstances, what emotions would surface? With what thoughts would you wrestle?

Fear? Of course you would.

Anxiety? To say the least.

Anger? I could understand that (you'd like to get your hands on those folks who convinced you to take this trip)

But most of all what about hopelessness? No idea where to turn. No hunch what to do. Who could blame you for sitting on a log (better check for snakes first), burying your face in your hands, and thinking, I'll never get of out here. You have no directions, no equipment, no hope.

Can you freeze frame that emotion for a moment? Can you sense, for just a second, how it feels to be out of your element? Out of solutions? Out of ideas and energy? Can you imagine, just for a moment how it feels to be out of hope?

If you can, you can relate to many people in this world.

For many people, life is – well, life is a jungle. Not a jungle of trees and beasts. Would that it were so simple. Would that our jungles could be cut with a machete or our adversaries trapped in a cage. But our jungles are comprised of the thicker thickets of ailing health, broken hearts and empty wallets. Our forests are framed with hospital walls and divorce courts. We don't hear the screeching of birds or the roar of lions, but we do hear the complaints of neighbours and the demands of bosses. Our predators are our creditors, and the bush that surrounds us is the rush that exhausts us.

It's a jungle out there.[1]

Can you identify with this feeling of lostness in your own life? Of not knowing which way to turn to get yourself back on track? Of being surrounded, even by people, and yet feeling very alone? No guide, no comfort, no anything, and especially no hope. Lucado suggests that we need three things: a *person to follow* and one who posseses both *vision* and *direction*. He concludes, "If you have only a person but no renewed vision, all you have is company. If he has a vision but no direction, you have a dreamer for company. But if you have a person with vision and direction – who can take you from this place to the right place – ah, then you have one who can restore your hope."[2]

The Bible gives us multiple evidence that God is both the guide we seek – *"The Lord is my Shepherd"* – and the company we need – *"I will never leave you."* Jesus says of Himself, *"I am the way."* How comforting is that?

"But, I'm lost," you say. "What you say sounds good, but I can't see the wood for the trees. I don't know which way to turn!"

We can feel afraid and anxious, even be paralysed by fear, but there are answers. We are pilgrims, we must keep moving forward. Some will protest, "But you don't know my past, my regrets, my wrong choices, my unhelpful words." No, but God does and He still loves you. If we look back over our life and find an ocean of regrets, what confidence can we have that when we look forward we won't be overcome with uncertainly about the future? We will look later in more detail at a promise God made to those needing guidance: "You will know which way to go even though you have never been this way before." The secret is: "His presence with and in you."

For others, the jungle is about the choices they must make. Sometimes we have too much information and at others, not enough. So many choices, too many decisions: Where? When? Who? Why? But still He says, "I will guide you."

Maybe your jungle is in your mind? If by training you are a scientist or a student of philosophy, then maybe God does not fit comfortably into your world of reason. You may be asking yourself, how can I keep my mind while making what seems like a leap of faith?

Yesterday I conducted the funeral of a friend, a member of the church I serve in. He died suddenly, only 60 years of age. I watched his widow and family amid obvious pain, sorrow and mourning, sing with great sincerity and unshakable belief some great hymns of our faith and I became very conscious that they knew the God who promises to *"comfort those who mourn."*

The difference is trust in Him / faith

Others, however, in times of unexplained loss can flounder. The jungle grows denser, the pain increases, the "whys" are unanswered. Blame and bitterness obscure the view and life closes in. What is it that makes the difference? It is the presence of God.

I may or may not have described your personal jungle, but whatever it looks and feels like, there is a way out, even if it is from desperate debt or dark despair. Max Lucado tells another jungle story,

> *The story is told of a man on an African safari deep in the jungle. The guide before him had a machete and was whacking away the tall weeds and thick underbrush. The traveller, wearied and hot, asked in frustration, "Where are we? Do you know where you are taking me? Where is the path?" And He, like the guide, doesn't*

tell us. Oh, He may give us a hint or two, but that's all. If He did, would we understand? Would we comprehend our location? No, like the traveller, we are unacquainted with this jungle. So rather than give us an answer, Jesus gives us a far greater gift. He gives us Himself. He is the person you need. He has vision and knows the direction you should take. Trust Him.[3]

Crossing Over

The "jungle" that the children of Israel had to negotiate on their journey of discovery took several different forms. It started as a place of slavery and limitation when, after centuries, God sent a deliverer. That tale is known as the Exodus. Their next jungle was gentler, in fact it was often a desert! God miraculously fed and guided them for a generation in the wilderness, but they grumbled, made false gods and after some poor democratic decisions waited patiently for all the over 21s to die.

Then Moses, who was soon to die himself, told the people, *"You have stayed long enough at this mountain. Break camp and advance."* Where to? Well it depended on who you listened to. God said it was the land He had promised to their forefathers, a land flowing with milk and honey. The majority of the people said it was a land of giants, of enemies, a land that devoured those living in it.

In facing your personal jungle and coming to the realisation that you have "stayed here long enough", you will be able to "break camp" or "cross over" with more ease when you agree with God's assessment of the situation. God declares that He has a promised land for you – a place of purpose; a prepared place, tailor-made for you. There may well be difficulties to face, giants to overcome, but His presence with you will make all the difference to your journey.

The Bible makes it clear that Israel's journey took much longer than it should have. Maybe your journey, like mine, has taken longer than it should. Don't be discouraged by that. It took Israel forty years to complete a journey that, technically, could have been accomplished in two weeks (Deuteronomy 1:2-3).

But God was patient and they arrived in due time. As far as we have travelled, you and I are not yet the people God would like us to be. We don't know Him as well as we should and we are not as mature as we could be. But as true as that is, don't let it be the excuse that prevents you from crossing over, leaving where you are, breaking camp. One thing is sure, we will never arrive where we are meant to be until we leave where we are!

Breaking Camp

The Bible uses a number of pictures and phrases to describe the literal and spiritual journey of becoming who we were born to be; moving towards that place where we were always meant to live, knowing and being known by Him and moving from being immature "child heirs" (Galatians 4:1) to receiving all our promised land with the "full rights of sons" (Galatians 4:5).

In Deuteronomy 1 the picture is this potentially difficult and uneasy one of "breaking camp" (v6-8), of leaving the familiar and the known; deciding that we need to leave behind us things that were once useful and helpful; recognising that there was more unhelpful clutter assembled around our lives than we realised. What do we do with all of that? A skip and a spade please! But this can be an exciting time too, as well as painful or difficult.

New horizons are beckoning and we can still journey to that "better place" taking with us all of the truly treasured things we carry with us — reminders and markers of happy, holy days; tokens of God's past blessing in our lives.

It means a time of work, clearing and carrying; a season where everything is more unsettled than usual. Do you see the picture? If we are to reach our "promised land" and be, in a more powerful and defined way, "presence carriers", then the same principles will apply. Maybe you should stop right here and work through that breaking camp picture again and see if there are things, issues you should leave, bury, destroy or treasure more? *Selah.*

By way of a simple illustration, not long ago after a service, a man responded, speaking to me privately about something I had said. My words had triggered in him a realisation that he had never dealt with an understandably serious reaction to discovering that not only had his father deserted his family, but he was also a bigamist. The father was now dead and all this was a long time ago, but I urged him to find a quiet place, ask for God's help, and to speak out his forgiveness, without condoning what happened, leaving the debris at the cross. Once dealt with, I knew that he could enter into a new level of freedom.

Another picture comes from the prophet Isaiah. *"Forget the former things,"* he says, and *"do not dwell on the past"* (Isaiah 43:18). Isaiah points to the important role that our mind plays in breaking camp. How we train our minds is a very significant part of being whole, healthy, happy and "holding" more of God's presence. The Bible gives us some clear injunctions about guarding our hearts and renewing our minds. The picture is one of discipline. Isaiah's

This has held me back lots of times

audience were called to "forget". What were they supposed to be forgetting?

In this context, some of what needed to be forgotten was the good times of the past. Good times? Yes, because often the "good old days" restrict and limit our thinking regarding what may happen in the future. It is impossible to move forward when you are anchored to the past – even if much of it was good and helpful. What was useful then is not necessarily useful now. My father, among many, often used to say, "The last wave on the beach is the first to oppose the next wave coming in." We must guard against that happening through us, especially those of us who are a little older!

Isaiah's text goes on to say that God would do what He had done before: *"Make a way in the desert and streams in the wasteland"* (Isaiah 43:19). Let us not circumscribe how that can happen with our past thinking! If we explore the wider context of Isaiah, we will also reflect on the reality that they were called to forget the "bad" of the former things/times as well as the good. The nations were challenged about their idolatry and God's special people, Israel, were chastised for forgetting God and not calling on His name (Isaiah 43:22), even trusting in idols and other things.

I am jumping ahead now, but I pause to challenge myself and many other Christians leaders as to whether we have relied on our programmes more than His presence? ...our organisation and structure more than a dependence on the power of God? Have we become "experts" in the pulpit and, as such, relied more on the wrong gifts and experience; depended less on being and becoming significant "presence carriers"? I am sure that as I continue to write, I will be challenged again on this theme!

Returning to Isaiah's words, we too need to forget some of the good and the bad and not dwell on the past. How God will do what He will do in the future is His business. Suffice to say for us, we must be ready to work on His plan, co-operate with His ideas and carry His presence in order to see His kingdom come and *"the earth filled with the glory of God as the waters cover the sea"* (Habakkuk 2:14).

The Bible pictures of breaking camp and forgetting the former things help to bring into focus some of the actions required of us to be ready for what God wants to do in our lives. For Israel, the time finally came for the next generation to "cross over", to posses what God wanted them to possess, to "apprehend what they had been apprehended for". The history is messy, "mental" and mad, all at the same time.

Come with me and allow me some poetic licence in retelling the Joshua 3 account of how they finally left the wilderness and began to inherit what had been promised them many centuries before.

We will call the boy Joseph. He is around eight years old. Like most of the families his Granddad is dead, but he is glad his dad is holding his hand. As with many an eight-year old, he is full of questions, looking around at what he and his dad are involved in. You could be surprised he isn't asking more questions. There are many people, at least hundreds of thousands, almost certainly millions, but there are only two men in the whole crowd who are over sixty years old. Why?

At present something is happening and it seems to be both ordered and chaotic at the same time. They had had a very early start three days ago, when everybody had packed up camp and moved to be near the Jordan river. Now the people are camped in the Jordan valley, a depression many hundreds of feet below sea level, with a steep escarpment behind them. It is the time of year when the river Jordan floods. The snow on the northern mountains, such as Mt Hermon, has melted and as a result the river has overflowed its banks. It can be a mile wide at its worst. Now, official looking men are walking through the vast crowd giving strange orders. They are telling all the people to look for some men, dressed in special clothes, carrying a wooden box, covered with what looks like unusual clothes and skins.

When they see these men (the priests) and the box (the ark of the covenant) they are to, "move from your positions and follow it" while maintaining a distance of around half a mile. All the people were told to wash their clothes and remain calm and attentive to what was happening.

The leader, an older, powerful looking man called Joshua, gave an important speech to all the people, telling them what was going to happen. He confessed that, "the living God was among them"; that He would keep His promise and drive out all of their enemies. He told them to choose a leader from each of the groups and he made a daring prediction that when the priests stood in the flooded river, the water would open up and the people would walk across without getting wet.

The next day, the men appeared carrying the box and did no more than walk straight into the flooded river. On the other side of the river were people who did not want them to cross over; who were ready and prepared to kill them.

It was a very unwelcoming scene. The questions came rapidly: "Where are they going Dad? ...why are those men carrying that box and standing in the river? ...what's going to happen to us all?"

Looked at one way these events are exciting, different, unusual. Looked at another way they could be considered bizarre, laughable. Given as much preparation time as they'd had, one might think they would have come up with a better invasion plan than this.

Dad takes Joseph by the hand. "Let's go and sit in the shade for a few minutes, son, and I'll try to answer your questions. You don't remember Granddad. He would sometimes do just what we are doing now. He would sit down with me and tell me all the stories of how God helped our families escape from the country of Egypt, where we were slaves and life was very hard. He would talk about the night we crossed the Red Sea because of a miracle; how God fed us every day in the desert and protected us. I remember that part myself, of course."

"So son, God who helped Granddad in the past, will help us to see what He promised us so long ago come true. It's an exciting time, Joseph. You are going to say, 'I was there when what God promised actually happened!' So don't be afraid. God's presence is going ahead of us and we are going to the promised land. Everything is alright we will all be safe. Come on, let's go and see what's happening."

"Put me on your shoulders Dad," Joseph asks. "Quick, I can't see!"

Ahead of them there is a commotion, lots of noise, the people are excited. The priests have stood in the river. "Dad, it's amazing, the water is flowing away on the left side and ... wow! On the right side it's stopped flowing. People are saying that the water is piling up in a great heap way upstream!"

This part of the story ends with everybody crossing over onto dry ground and big rocks being lifted out of the river and piled together, so that the people will always remember what happened and never forget it.

Before drawing out some practical responses from this ancient story for our own crossing over, a few other reflections. God is a multi-generational God. The "passing down" of our stories is important in the walk of faith. Hearing from, being inspired by, and taking over the baton of those who have gone before is a transition-challenge for every succeeding generation.

The miracle-working God of yesterday has not changed, can be trusted, and will prove faithful to His promises in the future. Every generation of eight-year old Josephs needs to hear the stories of their fathers and cry out, *"Where are all those wonders that our fathers told us about?"* (Judges 6:13)

But back to our main theme. If breaking camp can be messy and forgetting the former things is an issue of disciplining our minds, what specific lessons can we appropriate from the Joshua 3 crossing over story?

1. First, we need to practice *hearing well*. The leaders of the day were told, *"Go through the camp and give orders to the people"* (Joshua 3:3). Good leaders can help to guide us; they will confirm what God is saying to us. Our responsibility is to

listen to and for the voice of God, then hear what He is saying and apply and obey what we're told to do. We will be helped in this task by keeping our hearts tender, our devotion deep and our lives uncluttered. We will look in more detail later at how we may limit the distractions and the unnecessary noise that can so easily drown out the voice of God.

2. We need to focus on *seeing*. *"When you **see** the ark..."* (Joshua 3:3). One of the great questions of the Bible is, *"What do you see?"* The oft-quoted Proverb is still true that, *"Without vision the people perish"* (Proverbs 29:18 KJV). We take care of our ability to see – we visit opticians, wear protective equipment – because we know our eyesight is precious. But what about our spiritual eyes? Elisha the prophet prayed, *"O Lord, open his eyes so he may see"* (2 Kings 6:7). We often miss what God is doing because of our lack of ability to discern the workings of an Almighty hand, even in the ordinary events of life. Too many of us are happy to accept that it was a coincidence, it just happened. My dear friend J. John says, "the more you pray the more co-incidences just happen!" We should all pray "Lord, open my eyes, I want to see all that you want me to see."

3. We need to *recognise* God's presence. This next stage in the people's progress had already been an important facet of their life in the desert. They only moved on in their journey when the visible tokens of God's presence, the cloud by day and the pillar of fire by night, moved. In Joshua 3 they were invited to look out for the ark of the covenant and follow it. It was the most holy symbol they had and it epitomised God living among them. The cover of the box was called a number of

things, including the "mercy seat", the place where once a year, a blood sacrifice for all the people's sin was sprinkled.

"When you see this... move out... and follow it" (3:3). They were following that which embodied both the presence of God among His people and also His covenant with them. It was a sign that God would surely fulfil the promises He had made. We should follow the presence of God with similar confidence.

4. *Watch for the presence carriers.* The Old Testament had a unique group of people who were privileged to carry the ark of the covenant. They were literally "presence carriers". Thankfully, the New Testament gives a much broader remit for presence carriers. Peter identifies all "who believe" as a holy priesthood (1 Peter 2:5) and John in his Revelation writes,

"...because you were slain and with your blood you purchased men for God from every tribe and language and people and nation. You have made them to be a kingdom of priests to serve our God, and they will reign on the earth." (Revelation 5:9-10)

This new community of priests can include you, and offers to all forgiven men and women the opportunity to know the presence of God both with them and living in them.

We should all aspire to be such presence carriers. We should also seek to get to know people who fit this description – people who, whenever you meet them, make you more conscious of God. They change the spiritual atmosphere

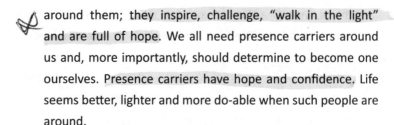 around them; they inspire, challenge, "walk in the light" and are full of hope. We all need presence carriers around us and, more importantly, should determine to become one ourselves. Presence carriers have hope and confidence. Life seems better, lighter and more do-able when such people are around.

5. *Always live where the presence of God dwells.* We are not called to celebrate the bizarre, the wacky, or people who, in a contrived way, just try to be different. But we should expect, while living a life of faith, keeping close to the presence of God, that sometimes unusual and unique challenges will come our way – like being asked to walk into a flooded river carrying a wooden box! If, in any season of your life, you struggle to discern and follow God's immediate presence yourself, then make sure you always have some reliable presence carriers who are accessible and can help you keep moving forward.

In this crossing over story, the presence of God was the most important thing. Your story may be different, mine certainly is, but the need for the presence of God remains central.

Before we move away from this story, two further thoughts to reflect on occur to me. The first is the amazing promise they were given and the second the provocative challenge they received.

The promise said, *"Then you will know which way to go, since you have never been this way before."* (Joshua 3:4). This truth resonates with other biblical declarations. For instance, *"If you acknowledge me in all your ways I will direct your paths"* (Proverbs 3:6) or *"Direct me in the path of your commands, for there I find delight"* (verse

39 of Psalm 119 which has many similar, potent statements). Jesus said, *"But seek first His kingdom and His righteousness and all these things will be given you as well"* (Matthew 6:33). So, keeping in step and in tune with the presence of God will give you a great assurance, as it did those ancient people. We can rest confident that we will know what we need to know, when we need to know it!

Even though our journey has unknowns and potential uncertainties, things are untried and we lack experience because we have never been here before, His promise is that *we will know.*

What about the challenge? First, it came with a breathtaking statement: *"Tomorrow the Lord will do amazing things among you"* (Joshua 3:5), so, *"consecrate yourself"*. This verse does not read, "If you ... then I will." It is a preparation not a precondition. So often in my decades as a Christ-follower, the concept and teaching of consecration was a demand, an obligation, a law. I would leave services feeling worse than I should, condemned by a "you must try harder" mentality.

In making this comment I am not for a moment encouraging a careless, sinful and undisciplined lifestyle, but I am urging you to see this consecration as a very positive, powerful and releasing challenge. The word-meaning includes the idea of something being "used for its designed purpose", and that to be used for anything less than God's will is profane. It becomes a very positive emotion, not so much what I must give up but what I will receive and enjoy – more of His presence. Not so much of being less, but of being more.

It has been well said that, "we must die before we can live, then we can live before we die." It is not a negative, but a wonderfully positive statement. If God asks for this consecration, He will give us the power and ability to be good, obedient disciples. It means that tomorrow our lives will be a precious perfume not a profane waste, and yes we could see things we have never seen before, amazing things!

It's time to step forward, leave the jungle, break camp, forget what needs to be forgotten and cross over. Whatever that means for you today, I urge you, take the next step. Don't wait any longer.

Today is the day of salvation.

2
Finding Alignment

I read this comment recently:

"In retrospect I can see in my own life what I could not see at the time; how the job I lost helped me find work I needed to do; and how the 'road closed' sign turned me toward terrain I needed to travel: and how losses that felt irredeemable forced me to discern meanings I needed to know. On the surface it seemed that life was lessening, but silently and lavishly the seeds of new life were always being sown."[4]

When we face situations like this in life we pray, we open the Bible, we share with trusted friends, because we believe we will arrive at the truth, especially in Scripture, and that *truth* has the power to set us free. The truth is, we can be free from whatever has limited, contained even "bugged" us for all or part of our lives. So how do we align ourselves with God so that we can truly receive His blessings?

We can think about a few simple parables that should help us get started. In the gates at the entrance to our previous family home was a substantial wooden letterbox to receive the mail. The box had a lock and my grandson, Edward, was very proud that he knew the combination of numbers that opened the lock. This is a form of "alignment".

A similar illustration finds you sitting at a computer, endeavouring to access some private information and you are nervous because you are not entirely sure which password you used to set up the account. Use the wrong one too many times and you will find yourself frozen out of the system you need to access.

The cricketer sweeps the ball to the boundary when balance, technique and timing combine together in alignment. If only one of those factors is wrong, he gives an easy catch.

The padlock on our old mailbox has 1,000 possible number sequences from 000 to 999, but only one (the one Edward knows!) opens the lock. It's the same with the right password and the cricketer. It's about alignment, having everything in the right place. With alignment everything seems easy!

That means, if we get ourselves in line with the purposes of God, things "open" to us. Things begin to happen that wouldn't otherwise happen. This is an exciting place to be. It is thrilling to be a presence carrier, to live with a sense of purpose and watch God at work doing amazing things. We must learn to be aligned to His plans and ways. That said, then what are some of the issues that hinder alignment and keep us out of line, not in the flow of His blessing? If and when we can identify a "problem", then we know what we must attend to if we are serious about our lives as devoted Christ-followers. The most obvious must be sin. Sin is a problem for all of us. Let us state some necessary facts:

We have all sinned and we still sin. John reminds us that, *"If we claim to be without sin we deceive ourselves and the truth is not in us"* (1 John 1:8). In case we didn't quite get the point the first time, he says in verse 10: *"If we claim we have not sinned, we make him out to be a liar and his word has no place in our lives."*

Thankfully, there is another fact sandwiched between these statements, that, *"If we confess our sins, He is faithful and just and will forgive our sins and purify us from all unrighteousness"* (v9). Another wonderful fact is that Jesus Christ has paid for every sin with His death on the cross. God the Father raised Him from death as an assertion of a "finished work". We still sin, but all sin is paid for. Does that mean we should be careless and indifferent about sin? Most certainly not. But should we live in denial about sin or condemnation for past sin? Also certainly not.

Before coming to faith in Christ the Bible says we were *"slaves to sin"*, but Romans 6:18 states that we have *"...been set free from sin and have become slaves to righteousness."* Now we have choices as to whether we sin or not. So let us make right choices, conscious that we still fail, but knowing that as *"we walk in the light the blood of Jesus is cleansing us from all sin."* My advice: repent quickly and always deal with sin urgently. If you are living in denial, know the conviction of the Holy Spirit about specific issues, or if you are aware of things that you have not repented of, come today to the cross, confess your sin and rise up forgiven and walk in the light. Sin, left un-dealt with, will keep us out of relationship with God. We will not be aligned for His blessing.

After sin, the next reality that helps or hinders our alignment is allowing Jesus to be Lord of our lives. Some of us are still fighting against becoming fully devoted followers of Jesus. Until we absolutely surrender every area of our lives to God and fully come under His Lordship, we are not in line for the full favour of God.

People tend to argue with God about how they use three things – their *time, talent* and *treasure*. The truth is, "we are not our own, we have been bought with a price." Our full freedom comes not only when we cease being slaves to sin, but when we choose to be "slaves to Christ". Does that mean we cannot make decisions about where we live or work or who are our friends? Of course not, provided we are surrendered to His ultimate Lordship, and that in all our choices we retain an inner knowledge of His peace – like an umpire guiding and confirming we are on the right path.

Many years ago I listened to a medical doctor who was working as a missionary in a hospital in Papua New Guinea. He expressed some fascinating thoughts and reflections on his life and missionary service. I will never forget one story.

He observed that some of the people who recovered quickest after hospital treatment had been to the witch doctor before attending the hospital. He made a more informed and scientific study to confirm his observations. Then, much to the surprise of some of his

Christian companions, he went to visit the witch doctor himself and asked him many questions about how he treated the sick before they came on to the hospital. I am conscious, as was he, that there is a darker side to the witch doctors "work", as with all forms of alternative spirituality, that is to be avoided.

He was, however, intrigued to find that the Shaman asked people about family, friends, broken relationship, things that they were bitter about, and issues of unforgiveness. The doctor concluded that when these primitive, animistic people attended to relationship breakdowns and inner issues to do with forgiveness, they were physically, emotionally and even spiritually better able to recover from their sickness.

The point this story plainly makes is that how we attend to our relationships is vitally important. Let me add, it also includes our attitude towards people who are already dead. I do not mean any attempt to connect with the dead, but rather whether we have unresolved issues of resentment, fear or unforgiveness that we still hold on to. Broken relationships damage us. Unforgiveness, anger and bitterness are all blockages that prevent the blessing of God flowing to us.

The Bible has many things to say about all these emotions and relational challenges, but I will highlight only one, because Jesus was specific and plain-speaking about it. He said,

"If you forgive men when they sin against you, your heavenly Father will also forgive you. But if you do not forgive men their sin, you Father will not forgive your sin." (Matthew 6:14-15)

Get ourselves right with God
to get into alignement
we have to let go of stuff
to recieve

He had already taught His disciples using a model prayer: *"Forgive us our debts, as we also forgive our debtors"* (Matthew 6:12). Lack of forgiveness damages our relationship with God, others and even ourselves. That makes dealing with it a serious matter.

I have heard numerous comments over years of Christian ministry: "How can I forgive them? ...but I have done nothing wrong, it's his problem ...well, I can't do anything about it now, she's dead and buried..." These are the sort of comments people make to excuse themselves from doing anything significant about expressing forgiveness.

The important point Jesus wants us to understand is the need for the correct, pro-active response, regardless of what has happened. He makes it clear that forgiveness will be necessary when we have been sinned against. Yes, the other person's actions and/or words were wrong and inappropriate – but that is not our issue. Proactive forgiveness is what is required of us if we want our lives rightly aligned to be conduits of God's blessing. It is not a case of, "When they say sorry, I'll say sorry." No, desiring true alignment requires us to act first.

Understanding this point means that it is unimportant whether the person is alive or dead. We still have a responsibility before God to express our forgiveness. I have found it particularly revealing when Christians are challenged about honouring their parents – an Old Testament command that carries a promise. Some people have told the most harrowing stories of betrayal, abuse, cruelty and abandonment and then ask, "How can I respect him?" Let me be absolutely clear about this. R. T. Kendall makes the point that releasing forgiveness to someone who has treated us appallingly does not mean we are "letting them get away with it", condoning their actions, or implying that what they did was okay. It was wrong and we cannot and should not ever "respect" such behaviour. But if we cannot honour our parents in the way they conducted themselves, we can at the very least obey the biblical mandate by "honouring" them for giving us life. Even this act has the power to release us from the bitterness and ongoing pain from such awful events.

If you need to, ask God to help you now and then speak out loud the words, "I forgive you." It may be appropriate to do this privately, with God, or it may be that you need to do it face to face with the person. Let God guide you in this.

I cannot stress enough the importance of forgiveness, nor adequately express its power to release those imprisoned by bitterness from the actions of others. I have seen amazing transformations take place in people's lives, often right in front of my eyes as a person has prayed and the Holy Spirit has touched that situation. Great burdens have been lifted off people's backs as years of inner turmoil have been gently lifted from them. It is wonderful to see. The underlying truth behind all of these thoughts is that the power of God flows in ways that are quite remarkable to us when we align ourselves to His word.

Let me recap on my postbox padlock. Edward knows the code and the lock opens. When we deal with sin, accept the Lordship of Jesus over our lives, and "straighten out" any relational wrangles, the numbers on life's lock are clicking into place. There is one more thought to share which will further aid our alignment!

People today have many fanciful ideas about what makes us, us! People say "you are what you eat". They debate over whether it is nature or nurture that shapes us as individuals. The Bible, however, makes one thing very clear: *"As a man thinks in his heart, so he is"* (Proverbs 23:7). *How* and *what* we think is the final alignment "lever" I would like us to think about.

Remember those ancient people coming out of Egypt, ready to possess their long promised inheritance? What did they think and say about themselves? They said, comparing themselves to the people who currently occupied the land, *"We seemed like grasshoppers in our own eyes, and we looked the same to them"* (Numbers 13:33). It is quite mesmerising to work out how they could possibly know what their enemies were thinking and saying!

Of course, they didn't know anything of the sort. Their wrong thinking and bad confession had brought a limitation to the fulfilment of their long-cherished dreams and aspirations. The wise words of the proverb I have just quoted tell us that it has ever been so. This is why the apostle Paul took so much time and effort to counsel us to "renew our minds" (see Romans 12:2, Philippians 4:8, Ephesians 4:23, 2 Corinthians 10:4-5). He taught that we need to straighten out our minds so as not to limit our own future, or as I taught in a sermon, your mind is your business, so mind your own business!

Some people think too much about themselves, are over-confident, self-sufficient and lack any dependence on God. Most, however, lack self-confidence and see themselves as unworthy. Their mantra is, "I'm not good enough!" – and this includes many highly gifted and already accomplished people. The great leader Moses said to

God, "Send my brother – I can't speak." Gideon hid when told that he was a mighty man of valour. Jesus, however, knew who He was, where He had come from, why He was here, what He was doing and where He was going. He was comfortable doing the lowliest servant's job whilst accomplishing the highest kingly task (John 13:1-17). Why? Because Jesus lived in the affirmation of His Father. He knew that He was accepted and loved by God and that He didn't need to strive to perform for Him in order to justify His existence. His thinking about Himself was perfectly aligned with God's word.

Let's be like Jesus. We must abandon all the negative words and stereotyping that our past life has imposed on us and be renewed in our thinking. We need to believe and confess that we are who God says we are. God says that we are, *"the apple of His eye"* (Zechariah 2:8; Deuteronomy 32:9-11), His *"treasured possessions"* (Exodus 19:5; Isaiah 43:2,4).

[handwritten marginal note, left: Rid old thinking + belief Systems]

[handwritten marginal note, right: we are new creations]

There are scriptures too numerous to relate here that tell us who we really are in Christ. Renewing our minds with these truths will heal and restore our broken identities and set us on the right track to accomplish all that God has planned for us. As we do this, dealing with the serious negatives that prevent us from being fully aligned to God's blessing, we can expect that blessing to increase.

Let me express this truth of alignment in a different way to reinforce the point and hopefully give you a positive perspective to help you hold your new found place of alignment. Paul writes, *"Therefore, if anyone is in Christ, he is a new creation, the old has gone, the new has come"* (2 Corinthians 5:17). He ends the same chapter with another remarkable statement:

"God made him [Jesus] *who had no sin to be sin for us, so that in Him we might become the righteousness of God."* (2 Corinthians 5:21)

In each of these verses is an "in" context. First, "in Christ" we are a new creation, then, "in Him" we become the righteousness of God. Our positional status is "in Christ" and "in Him". It is our responsibility to make that positional truth a practical day to day reality. Let me illustrate that from one specific perspective:

Most of us battle from time to time with one or all of the following emotional reactions to our sin, failure and inadequacy. We are gripped with fear, guilt, shame and condemnation – none of which are helpful, certainly do not come from God and which leave us limited, empty and weary. The verses we have just read say that in Christ we are new creations and have become the righteousness of God.

When we understand the power of these verses, we will realise that there is no place for fear, guilt, shame or condemnation, even in our times of weakness and failure. When God looks at you He sees His righteousness. Because you are in Christ, what He observes is you "hidden" in Christ. We are legitimately seen as "righteous" before God because of the divine exchange that takes place in our life as we identify with the finished work of Christ on the cross.

So fear, guilt, shame and condemnation have no place or hold over us. All the root issues that release these emotions are already dealt with. We are righteous, even more than forgiven. Dare we say it like that? Yes. Through Christ we are put in right standing with God, as though we had never sinned. Wow! Grasp this truth and you have positive ammunition for keeping your alignment to God's blessing. Here are a few scriptures to further help your confession and understanding.

1. About fear

"We are no longer slaves to fear … we receive the spirit of sonship." (Romans 5)

"There is no fear in love … perfect love drives out fear." (1 John 4:18)

2. What about guilt?

"Having our hearts sprinkled to cleanse us from a guilty conscience." (Hebrews 10:22)

"God convicts us with a solution: to wash us clean, never to leave us feeling guilt." (John 16 The Message)

3. How about our shame?

"The one who trusts in Him [Jesus] will never be put to shame." (1 Peter 2:6)

4. Condemnation

And finally, powerful words from Paul's Roman treatise that deals with condemnation: *"Therefore there is no condemnation for those who are in Christ Jesus."* (Romans 8:1)

Aligning ourselves with the truth of God's word will counteract the things that try to rob us of our identity in Christ. Ask God now for a new level of revelation and understanding of what it means to be *"in Christ"* and what the full blessing of *"being the righteousness of*

God" could and should mean to you. It will at least mean a happy goodbye to fear, guilt, shame and condemnation. So let's thank God for that.

The final point of alignment I need to make is associated with how we deal with the changing circumstances and events that occupy our daily lives – that lost job, the "road closed" sign of the opening quote in this section of the book. I have said a thousand times, "It is not what happens to you that matters, but how you react to what God knows is happening to you that matters."

When we read the emotionally draining account of Jesus praying in the garden of Gethsemane, we are impressed by His commitment to His father. His prayer is deeply relational – *"Abba Father"*, then confessional – *"everything is possible for you"*, continuing with an emotional petition – *"take this cup from me"* and is finally submissive – *"yet not what I will, but what you will."* This is a wonderful example of how we should align ourselves with God's will, whatever the circumstances of life. We submit: "Not my will, but yours."

This stance keeps us in the centre of God's will and purpose whether each day is pleasant or painful, understood or unknown. We come to God as our Abba; we believe that all things are possible with Him; we honestly express our desires and then in everything commit to do His will. A Bible school motto I remember was, "To be in your will is better than success". I would prefer to say, "To be in your will *is* success."

We pause for a breather. We have viewed a land where the Abba of Jesus waits, looks and longs for an intimate relationship with each of us. We pass through our "jungles" and remove and overcome the obstacles that limit our enjoyment of His presence. Then, we learn from the ancient people Israel:

"These things happened to them as examples and were written down as warnings for us..." (1 Corinthians 10:11).

We break camp and cross over, facing the unknown and uncertain with confidence, because His presence brings the assurance that we will "know which way to go". This part of our "spying out the land" has focused on dealing with the negatives and embracing the positives that help or hinder our alignment to being the presence carriers our souls long to be. Now onward! What more can we learn from all our yesterdays?

3
Lessons From History

I am very conscious as I write, that whilst it is appropriate to state and even re-state past learnings from my own journey of faith – and I will – there is a stronger urgency to explore what we can learn about enjoying the presence of God from other historical contexts, both ancient and modern.

How do we help each other find an honest assessment of both our journey of faith and enjoyment or otherwise of the presence of God? Let me speak briefly about the "faith" part. Have we even started to trust God that He has a unique purpose for each and all of us? Or did we, in a past season, start on such a journey but now we have stopped, become side-tracked or even stuck and may not have even realised it? You may humbly know that you are most definitely not in either of those categories, but are grateful to be poked with a stick called truth about the journey still to be undertaken, the ground to be gained and the prize yet to be enjoyed. Wherever we are on this journey, we will be helped by reminding ourselves of the need to embrace change, to take a risk, to escape from survival thinking, to leave behind immaturity, remembering the past and embracing the present – following God's leading with zeal and passion. But at this moment I am urged to explore how strong is our desire to know more of God's presence? I will return to these "reminders" later in the chapter.

In my lifetime, I have watched individuals and groups move from a radical, risk-taking spirituality to a traditional, limiting and tired expression of faith. Others have made the reverse journey from a tired and traditional faith to a vibrant, renewed one. Movements that began when people discovered a new revelation of truth have become controlled organisations, sometimes brutalised by legalism and now limited by rules and by-laws. Others have faded into insignificance and irrelevance, not realising that "the glory has departed". How does this happen? Are the people involved bad or ill-intentioned? Almost exclusively the answer is no. Rather, we seem to set up camp around what we know and experience. We lose our appetite for challenge and risk. We become comfortable and content and stop seeking God with the hunger we once had. A.W. Tozer uses very similar language when writing about two kinds of ground from Hosea 10:12, which says, *"Break up your fallow ground."*

"God works as long as His people live daringly: He ceases when they no longer need His aid. As soon as we seek protection out of God, we find it to our own undoing. Let us build a safety-wall of endowments, by-laws, prestige, multiplied agencies for the delegation of our duties, and creeping paralysis sets in at once, a paralysis which can only end in death."[5]

The history of the Christian faith has many illustrations of such a decline. From the last century, the Pentecostal revival with its renewed view of the work of the Holy Spirit continues apace around the globe. But in some of its most organised forms it is over-structured and tired. The later Charismatic renewal is vibrant and growing in parts and forgotten in others. We can comment on our longer history. How did what Wesley achieved and believed become most of Western Methodism today? The same could be said of Luther's movement, and on and on. Even deeply spiritual communities going back to the desert fathers have seemed to falter and stumble, allowing themselves to be trapped in too narrow an expression of spirituality and understanding of truth.

Are there any common factors throughout this long history? It may be over simplifying things to say – but I still believe it is true – that a loss of the presence of God and a lack of dependence upon Him are at the heart of the problem. How then shall we learn, in these early years of a new century? We must realise that however successful we look now, however well organised we are, and even with significant resources, without the presence of God our days are numbered.

Please hear me. I am most certainly not having a cheap shot at any or all of the mega-church, brand-style, attractional congregations or networks. I am thankful for every group, large or small, well known or not, who are faithfully bringing lost people to Christ and seeing broken lives made whole. I am simply concerned that we learn from history – something we don't do easily or well – that without a dependence on God (that means it won't work without Him) and an active hunger for His presence, as individuals and in whatever grouping we find ourselves, our effectiveness will be short lived. There are many church meetings one can attend where the level of professionalism is unquestioned, the enthusiasm is infectious and the people involved are committed and sincere. But where is that tangible awareness that God is in His house?

Let us now look much further back to a time when Moses met God and two generations of amazing and awful things happened side by side. Maybe there are a few key principles and lessons that we would be wise to learn. If the relevance of the Exodus temporarily escapes you, allow me to remind you. No one in the nation of Israel could remember what it was like to live as a free man or woman. They were slaves and their pain had gone on a long time. Pause to look around the so called First World, the rich West, the "old Christian" countries and what do we see? – a very similar picture.

Thankfully, there are pockets of light and spiritual vitality, but there are also hundreds of millions of people living without God and with very little hope. Lives trivialised by getting, greed, entertainment, and lulled by sport and pleasure. Jesus spoke about a culture dead to spiritual reality when He said, *"We played the flute for you and you did not dance, we sang a dirge and you did not mourn"* (Matthew 11:17). In another place, the culture of the day was summarised by the words, *"Eat, drink and be merry for tomorrow we die"* (1 Corinthians 15:32). The world that Moses was thrust into, like our world and especially the West, was desperately in need of something spiritual and special.

Moses was something of a confused man. He was born into a Hebrew family and, at a time when all male offspring of the Hebrews were being slaughtered, he was miraculously protected. He then grew up effectively living as an Egyptian prince, but was disturbed by issues of justice and social concern and took the law into his own hands. Forced to flee all that he knew and after years as a fugitive, now living as a "Bedouin tribesman", he became intrigued by a strange sight and heard God speak. It isn't long into this unusual encounter before he asks the Almighty, *"Who am I?"* (Exodus 3:11)

God commissioned Moses at that moment. We are familiar with the story. Moses is given a clear strategy, backed up with miraculous support and, after a titanic struggle, God's people are free and back on track to inherit their promised land and do His bidding. The unfolding history has many facets. I will amplify one, for it contains the point of my writing. Their journey was not straightforward. No self-respecting Sat Nav would have taken them the route they went. But, *"God led the people…"* and *"by day the Lord went ahead of them in a pillar of cloud to guide them on their way and by night in a pillar of fire to give them light"* (Exodus 13:18, 21). In the next chapter the presence moves to become protection, standing between them and their enemies (Exodus 14:19-20). Later, after an idolatrous rebellion, Moses again speaks with God:

"You have been telling me, 'Lead these people,' but you have not let me know whom you will send with me." (Exodus 33:12)

He asks God to, *"teach me your ways, so I may know you and continue to find favour with you"* (v13). The Lord's reply was all he needed: *"My presence will go with you, and I will give you rest"* (v14). In an earlier conversation, God had said He would send an angel with them, but would not go with them Himself because they were stiff-necked and stubborn. Moses' response to the Lord's "changed" plan was essentially, "Good! Because if you aren't with us then please don't send us anywhere!" (v15). He then asks a profound and important question: *"What else will distinguish me and your people from all the other people on the face of the earth?"* (v16).

The conclusion we draw from this conversation is that the presence of God is a sign of Him being pleased with us and that His presence with us is the one thing that makes us different. Moses continued with many private meetings with the Lord. Joshua was also often there and would sometimes stay after Moses had left. These encounters became so powerful that Moses' face literally changed. It was radiant, bright, vibrant. The New Testament describes this as the effect of "glory" (2 Corinthians 3:7).

Later, God instructed them to build a "tabernacle" to house His presence. It has long fascinated me that something so small could play such a major part in the nation's life. The tabernacle was 15m x 5m (45ft x 15ft) and the whole enclosed space approximately 50m x 25m (150ft x 75ft). Yet in a city of 2-3 million people it dominated their lives. The book of Exodus ends with Moses, who knew about the glory of God, unable to go into this space because the presence of God was so intense.

We could spend time looking at myriad other amazing events: the plagues, the red sea crossing, the daily manna, the water from the rock, the ground opening up in judgement, and so on. They all happened because of the overriding and supreme reality that God was with them. It was a meeting with God that changed everything for both Moses and the people. It was a promise from God that guaranteed everything and it was the presence of God that brought their deliverance and eventually transported them to the promised land.

What simple truths can we learn from this much-edited story?

1. Moses was curious about the supernatural – "I will go over and see this strange sight – why the bush does not burn up."
2. Moses discovered his **identity** in the presence of God - "I am the God of your father..."
3. Moses received **a promise** in the presence of God – "I will be with you."
4. Moses received **a strategy** in the presence of God – "I am sending you to Pharaoh to bring my people the Israelites out of Egypt."
5. Moses was **supported by miracles** from the presence of God – "I will stretch out my hand and strike the Egyptians with all the wonders that I will perform among them..."
6. Moses **learned protection** in the presence of God – "The cloud moved..."
7. Moses **increased in dependence** on God – "If you don't go with us..."
8. The Lord would speak with Moses **face to face** (Exodus 39:11).
9. Moses used to take a tent ... calling it the **"tent of meeting"** (Exodus 33:7).
10. Moses **knew more of the presence** of God – "they saw that his face was radiant."
11. Moses could not enter the tent ... the glory of the Lord filled the Tabernacle (Exodus 40:34).

[handwritten margin note: what a process! a presence carrier goes through in order to reach ...]

12. Joshua learned early **the importance of the presence** of God:
    "but his young assistant Joshua son of Nun did not leave the
    tent."

Fast forward the time tape. Dwelling on the truths contained in this
story we can ask ourselves, "How are we doing?" Are we hungry for
more of God's presence? Are we more, rather than less, dependent
on Him than we have been before in our lives? Are we secure in
Him because of increased time spent in His presence? Or are we
too consumed with work and general busyness to spend "proper"
time with God? As a result, have we maybe even forgotten some of
His precious promises to us?

Surveys reveal horrible statistics of how little time many Christian
leaders spend in prayer and mediation, how little of Scripture many
Christians know and how estranged we have become from knowing
"the ways of the Lord". Maybe we need to hear again the message
of the officials in the crossing-over story of Joshua 3: look for the
ark – the presence of God – and follow the presence carriers. If
things have become stale for you, move your position, change your
routine, be excited about moving forward in the unknown of the
purpose of God for you, your family and the Christian community
in which you play a part. Hear the words again: "consecrate
yourselves".

Remember this is not some work of dutiful, disciplined obedience,
but a positive hunger to know God afresh; to not waste our time and
gifts on lesser things which the Bible calls profane. Duty and discipline
will turn to delight when we meet God in a new way, hear His loving
voice and see His beauty in the face of Christ. A new dependence on
knowing and being with Him will impact everything in our lives.

Is it time to stop, reading at least, and maybe to "stop" in a more profound way? Be still for a moment. Close down the outside noise and find a place of inner quiet. It is sometimes harder than we think it should be, especially if we haven't practiced for a long time. For some of us, a driving compulsion needs to be stilled – the busyness that Hilary of Tours referred to as, "a blasphemous anxiety to do God's work for Him." Now focus on Jesus. Let a Bible promise rise up in your spirit and enjoy being with the Lord. As I have obeyed my own words and stopped I heard, "I will never leave you or forsake you." How wonderful is that? This "practice" may take a few moments, but given time it will turn into a full blown encounter with God. This should be a part of our daily spiritual walk – to be alert to, tuned into the voice of the Holy Spirit; aware of God's abiding presence. Here is a prayer I sometimes pray that has helped me on this journey:

"Lord, grant me the grace to do one thing at a time today, without rushing or hurrying. Help me to savour the sacred in all I do, be it large or small. By the Holy Spirit within, empower me to pause today as I move from one activity to the next. In Jesus' name. Amen." (The Daily Office, p16)

It is a matter for the Holy Spirit to help each of us to determine when and whether more time is needed to attend to His deeper promptings. If you know that your priorities need to change, that significant time issues must be faced, then do what is necessary. Please don't procrastinate. It is too important and maybe, like Moses, the whole course of your life could change if you will turn aside and deal with the Spirit's prompting.

Now let us return to the issues I mentioned at the beginning of this chapter. These are the issues each of us desiring to break camp and move on need to deal with:

1. Embrace Change

The necessity to embrace change was an important part of Israel's story. They needed to change their thinking, their actions and their language more than once. After 400 years as slaves, the nomadic people of the wilderness were free, but not "home". Flushed with the wealth of Egypt (was it four hundred year's wages in a night?!) they had to stop living, thinking, acting and speaking like slaves and live as free men and women. Later, when they crossed the Jordan, it all changed again. No longer was food provided by miracle manna, but they needed to work, dig the ground, sow seed and enjoy the harvest.

Our lives, like theirs, can change overnight, for God's nature and power are still the same. Our responsibility is to adapt and to embrace change when the crossing over season comes.

2. Take a risk and set out

As they entered the wilderness, Israel's thinking changed from, "Get me out of here" to "Please and thank you". Life had suddenly become comfortable as all their needs were catered for. Often we lapse into presumption, like they did, rather than being thankful.

The wilderness is not the place of arrival, however, but of transition. We need to take a risk and move on. 500 years ago Columbus risked disaster, ignominy and death, but he discovered a new world. Accepted wisdom said that he would sail his boat over the edge of the world, but he sailed it to a new one. God says to you, as you obey Him, it's time to sail where you've never been before and discover that He has a new world for you. Why should it be the next generation of your family, business or church that breaks out of survival and not you? Why not you and why not now? Break out from limitation and past failure and possess your promised land.

3. Escape from survival thinking

I read a sad but funny story recently. It was about two old men who had feuded for years. One is now dying and good sense prevails, so forgiveness is sought and found. But then the old man tells his former enemy, "If I recover, the feud is back on!" How slow we are to learn. So often we don't know how to change our survival thinking and deal with what ruins us. Survival is more comfortable than slavery, but it is not where we are meant to live.

In a recent Sunday morning service Kate took the microphone during the worship time and shared a powerful story. She was twenty-three when her mother died in a road accident. She was devastated. When attending services she would sing, "You are my shield, strength, fortress and my help," but found it difficult to believe those words. Many years later, however, she understands how true those words are and says, "To anyone still bearing the pain of questions and loss, keep singing what is true and eventually it will work for you."

Jesus came out of His wilderness in the power of the Spirit and He invites us to come out of ours. Stop being only a survivor, blaming your circumstances and in crossing over, take hold of all that is available to you in Christ – especially the promise of His continuing presence with you. Remember, every saint has a past and every sinner has a future.

4. Leave behind immaturity

Galatians speaks of those who are meant to be fully responsible heirs still being like children (Galatians 4:1). The root word behind "child" here includes the thought of a babbling one, still an infant, not yet fully developed. The children of Israel were slow to mature. They had good leadership, but did not grasp the importance of taking responsibility for their own development. It is the same for us. In the desert there were no giants to kill, no seeds to sow. It was a glorified social welfare programme. They had little responsibility. We, like them, cannot live forever as consumers, rather than providers, living reactive instead of pro-active lives.

We are here for a purpose. There is a mission to complete. Crossing over then, is not just about leaving behind sin and bondage, but also about taking responsibility for our lives – and that may mean leaving behind comfort, ease and complacency or whatever God is shining His light onto in our lives.

5. Remember the past

It is one of the many ironies and paradoxes of the Bible that we are to both forget and remember the past. For Israel it was to forget the slavery and remember the deliverance. Millennia later, at the heart of the Jewish year and culture is the Passover. For us as Christians we must take heed to Jesus' words reported by Paul: *"Do this in remembrance of me"* (1 Corinthians 11:24-25). In many Christian communities this is not done very often. I don't understand why not. Of course our remembering is more than breaking bread – our sharing communion or celebrating the Eucharist, to use broad language. We should remember and rehearse God's goodness with testimony and storytelling all the time. It has an amazing impact. We call a part of our life as a congregation in Nottingham, "celebrating home" – telling the stories of what God is doing in the church's many ministries. It is hard to quantify the impact of those times, especially in staff meeting sessions. Sometimes, after half an hour of stories, the faith level rises, the encouragement is electric and the togetherness felt. It is because we remember. Back to breaking bread briefly: alongside whatever formal context you celebrate and enjoy, be encouraged to informally remember. Around a family meal table, in a restaurant with friends, a picnic or a barbecue, break bread, stop and be thankful. It will have a powerful impact.

6. Embrace the presence

After an enjoyable and engaging conversation about angels in an Elder's meeting we began a time of prayer. At one point the room fell silent and the manifest presence of God enveloped us. We are always in God's presence, but sometimes it intensifies. When He is "here" anything can happen. Whatever else is going on in our lives, the most important thing is for us to develop an unquenchable desire for more of these manifest moments where we know, as more than a theory, that He is with us.

Exodus 23:20-31 shows us that this presence can both protect and direct us, sending an angel ahead of us *"to guard you along the way ... pay attention and listen to what he says."* God promises to guard the people and guide them, to bring them to the place He's already prepared. The more of His presence we know, although we are going where we've never been before, yet we will know where to go.

7. Follow God's lead

If studied on a map, the route Israel took across the desert was not the way we would plan a journey. I would want to get there quickly, A to B, not go on a circuitous route. Yet the Bible says God was leading them.

We many not understand why we are where we currently are, but we need to have a deep and abiding faith that God is leading us. He had a reason to take Israel the route He did. He is not duty bound to tell us all the reasons why!

God manifest Himself in a cloud and a pillar of fire – two manifestations that helped Israel to keep moving forward, day or night. The presence of God in you will help you move when you need to move. Circumstances have nothing to do with it. When the "cloud" or the "fire" moves, we follow.

As a church we bought some land nearly twenty years ago, because we felt strongly it was what God wanted us to do. There have been many twists and turns in the road since that time. As I write there are significant developments and maybe the time for the land to yield its harvest is upon us. Maybe it will release resources for us or maybe there is yet another turn in the road. We must continue to obey and trust, even when we don't seem to be on the most direct route. Being confident in knowing the voice of God and exercising faith and trust for however long will keep us in the centre of God's plan and purpose – and that is the best place to be.

It is time to stop and reflect. What thinking do you need to change? What immaturity should be left behind? What risks should be undertaken? Where is God asking you to follow His lead? When we realign our thinking and actions with God's, we can become all we were born to be, consciously enjoy more of His presence, and live fulfilled and fruitful lives. This is a message filled with hope and incredible possibilities. Let us learn from history, including our own, and face the future with confidence and any challenges with faith and fortitude.

4
The Challenge

There is a massive political project marching across Europe – the European Union. It has many parts and stirs many, sometimes extreme, emotions of both support and hatred. Whenever the negative challenges become strong, one of the foundational arguments for its continuance is that we must not go back to the days of warring nations and world wars with their unspeakable suffering, pain and evil. However flawed, it's a human reaction to the horrors of war.

There is another more massive project abroad in the earth called the Kingdom of God, where a titanic struggle (even a war) continues for the destination of the souls of men and women and a daily battle ensues to limit every human from reaching their God-given potential – which includes knowing and carrying the presence

Gods needing more to set our attention to seek him

of God. This struggle is illustrated throughout the pages of Bible history and I observe the same repeating challenges in my own life and that of most of the people I know. It is horrible to see the effects of the "serpent's" work and then glorious to see the Saviour transform a life, making it like Christ. I will pick out several biblical characters whose challenges in life illustrate the nature of the battle we face to become who God intends us to be. They are instructive because they highlight the critical issues of character development we all have to negotiate. Plus, we must learn to recognise and combat the devices that our enemy consistently and persistently applies to stop us.

The Garden

All is perfection; it is the garden of Eden. In this perfect world man has work to do (decided by God), relationships to develop – one with God and another with his "help mate" – and a moral code to obey. The first full day of man's consciousness on earth is a day of rest and not labour. What a great start and a revelatory truth that most of us have missed – we rest from work, they worked from rest. Our frequent slackness in this area leaves us more vulnerable than we need to be and more open to sin and failure.

What more can we learn? Well the serpent *undermined the voice and word of God*: "Did God really say...?" he said to Eve, and he says the same thing to us today, seeking to undermine and deceive. The woman misread what she saw. *"It was pleasing to the eye ... and desirable for gaining wisdom"* (Genesis 3:6). Our eye can often mislead us. Adam and Eve were offered something they already possessed, but did not appreciate. "You will be like God," insisted the deceiver – yet they already were! Following on from their disobedience their perfect world was turned upside-down, they were put out of the garden, and they no longer enjoyed the same intensity of God's presence they were created to enjoy. We need to come to a place where we trust God's word and trust His leading. He knows what we need better than we know ourselves. Don't allow sinister, undermining words from an enemy to sneak in and rob you of your destiny.

The Dreamer

One of the early dreamers of the Bible was Joseph. He overcame herculean obstacles that were attempting to divert him from fulfilling his dream as a presence carrier and a man of purpose. His journey alerts us to the challenges we are likely to face.

His enemies – his brothers in the flesh, but who knows the identity of his unseen spiritual opposition – first tried to CRUSH his dream, mocking his confession: *"Will you actually rule us?"* Then they tried to CONFUSE him, taking his robe from him and throwing him in a well. Then, prevented from actually killing him, they sold him as a slave, trying to CONFISCATE his identity. But amidst all his troubles (and they were long and many) the Bible keeps telling us that, *"The Lord was with him."*

Next came the plan to COMPROMISE him. Day after day, a wealthy woman offered him "easy" sex. In the end he fled, leaving his cloak behind in order to keep his integrity. It cost him an unjust prison sentence, but he retained the presence of God. Now cruelly deprived of his freedom his enemies are trying to CONFINE him. What a journey! Joseph had been robbed of his symbolic coat – the garment that expressed his specialness and favour – and was now wearing prison clothes because, to preserve his character, he had surrendered his cloak. After a year or two of further disappointment, however, this man's character had been shaped and honed by God to such an extent that he was ready to be thrust onto the world stage, see his dreams fulfilled, become an economic wizard and a international deliverer, always knowing that, *"The Lord was with him"*.

Which part of history must you and I most take to heart, so that on the road to our dream we are not side-tracked and fall short of our best possibilities?

The Shepherd King

Then we have the example of the initially successful shepherd-king, David. With the help of a little courage and the assurance of the strength of his God, David fought and defeated lions, bears and the Philistine giant Goliath – all before he was even shaving properly! But unlike Joseph, David learned through personal failure and sin that he could still enjoy the presence of God, despite the circumstances of his life. Read slowly with me the heart-rending, yet hope-restoring language of Psalm 51:1-12:

"Have mercy on me, O God, according to your unfailing love; according to your great compassion blot out my transgressions. Wash away all my iniquity and cleanse me from my sin. For I know my transgressions and my sin is always before me. Against you, you only, have I sinned and done what is evil in your sight, so that you are proved right when you speak and justified when you judge. Surely I was sinful at birth, sinful from the time my mother conceived me. Surely you desire truth in the inner parts; you teach me wisdom in the inmost place. Cleanse me with hyssop, and I shall be clean; wash me, and I shall be whiter than snow. Let me hear joy and gladness; let the bones you have crushed rejoice. Hide your

face from my sins and blot out all my iniquity. Create in me a pure heart, O God, and renew a steadfast spirit within me. Do not cast me from your presence or take your Holy Spirit from me. Restore to me the joy of your salvation and grant me a willing spirit, to sustain me."

Here is a man owning up to his moral failure, not hiding anything. "Blot out *my* transgression, wash away all *my* iniquity, cleanse me from *my* sin. Then he petitions God: *"Cleanse me ... wash me ... hide your face from my sin ... create in me a pure heart."*

Why? Because he longs to be consciously aware again of God's presence as he was when singing his love songs and the psalms of his youth. He still remembered what joy and delight it brought.

Over the years of my life I have prayed this prayer of David's many times, especially in those moments when, for whatever reason, I have been conscious of God's displeasure with my words, thoughts or actions. When the joy has gone, the peace of God is hard to find and we feel unwashed, what ecstasy it is to know forgiveness and freedom, to be confident that we are the righteousness of God in Christ and that He is with us, living in us.

As I sit writing I am urged to express the pain I feel for those who, like David, have made very public mistakes; who have failed morally and probably lost many things including a present experience of God's presence and a fresh anointing of His Spirit. If this describes you in any measure, whoever you are and wherever you live, pray again and find again, as David did, the joy of your salvation. Ask God to guide you to someone you can pray with and find restoration.

So, Adam and Eve gave something away, Joseph overcame to persevere and walk with God and David lost and re-found his place in God. What about Elijah, another success story? What a man – the rain maker! The destroyer of idolatry and the man whose prayer brings fire from heaven and who runs faster than a racing horse and chariot. There is something very special about this prophet. After such heroic success and faced by the threat of an idolatrous queen he runs for his life in a suicidal depression, telling God, "I want to die." God miraculously looks after him, builds up his strength and helps him rest – both very important things to remember when under fire and feeling the pressure. Then, in a unique way, God speaks to him again.

Our English Bibles use the language of a "gentle whisper" (1 Kings 19:12), but a clearer meaning is that God speaks to him "in the silence". I will reflect more in a later chapter about this silence. God asks Elijah, "What are you doing here?" – a very good question God sometimes asks us, designed to cut to the heart of our motives. Then the Lord tells him to, "Go back the way you came." In other words, go and release a new future, set people apart, anoint them.

What can we learn from Elijah? Certainly that we should be vigilant against attack, especially after times of success. Maybe we should also watch out for intimidation, loss of strength and over tiredness. Sometimes we will need to hear God's voice in the silence and go back the way we came, find and re-use the lost axe-head (2 Kings 6:6) and, to change the metaphor, do some baton passing to the next generation.

The pages of history turn and we meet Jesus in the gospels. I hasten to add, He is not the next one in a list of ordinary people we learn from in the same way as we learn from the lives of others. He is God in the flesh, completely "other", unique, captivating and the example we follow. Having laid aside the advantage of deity for a season, as Philippians 2 poignantly teaches, He passed through many tests and trials. Before the cross He confesses, *"For the prince of this world is coming. He has no hold on me"* (John 14:30). He has overcome every challenge and is able to offer His life as the perfect substitute and sacrifice for all sin.

At the beginning of Jesus' ministry the text speaks of Him receiving His Father's approbation and blessing and of the Holy Spirit descending on Him like a dove. Then Luke 4 says He was, *"full of the Spirit"* and *"led by the Spirit into the desert."* This Spirit-filled and Spirit-led man is tempted for 40 days before "returning" to Galilee in the power of the Spirit. Then, in Luke 4:14, He is in the synagogue where He confesses, *"The Spirit of the Lord is on me."* For all who were present that day it must have been an unforgettable experience.

We can only conclude that Spirit-filled and Spirit-led men and women will face fierce opposition and tough times, including challenges to who we are, who and what we worship, and who we trust and depend on. The Old Testament makes it clear that, "all anointed people are attacked" (2 Samuel 5:17). We need to know, as Jesus did, how to use the Scriptures as the sword of the Spirit and learn to overcome. Then we will maintain His presence in Spirit-filled lives, know God's approval and fulfil His plan and purpose.

Later in Luke's gospel chapter 22 the words of Jesus give us another insight. He is answering a dispute that has broken out among the disciples as to who among them is the "greatest" – the most important. This dispute is a reoccurring theme in every generation. Jesus instructed them, and instructs us, not to be like the community around them.

"Instead, the greatest among you should be like the youngest and the one who rules like the one who serves." (v26)

Jesus speaks of being an example to them: *"I am among you as one who serves"* (v27), then recognises that His disciples are, *"those who have stood by me in my trials"* (v28) and then speaks of their place in the coming kingdom. In verses 31 and 32 He provides three further insights. Speaking of Peter He says,

1. "Simon, Simon, Satan has asked to sift you as wheat..."
2. "But I have prayed for you, Simon, that your faith will not fail..."
3. "When you have turned back, strengthen your brothers."

Let's briefly look at these statements. Peterson, in The Message writes, *"Simon, stay on your toes, Satan has tried his best to separate all of you from me, like chaff from wheat."* Among the tests and trials of life, Jesus is making it clear to Peter and us that the devil's significant aim is separation and division – however he can cause it, but chiefly by us being separated in our relationships with Jesus Himself. So we must be alert, on our guard for his evil tricks.

We can find huge consolation in the fact that the Great Intercessor knows us all by name and is praying for us, specifically that our faith will not fail. I am always hugely comforted when I read or reflect on the words of Hebrews:

"Since we have a great high priest who has gone through the heavens, Jesus the son of God, let us hold firmly to the faith we profess" (Hebrews 4:14).

Finally, after our tests and trials we are able to strengthen and comfort others. Like precious metal refined in the heat of a furnace, something happens to us and in us when we face our trials that cannot be produced in any other setting or context. We are made stronger to encourage and strengthen others.

The challenge I have endeavoured to highlight in this chapter is clear and straightforward. You will not enjoy a continuing and growing relationship with God, consciously knowing His abiding presence, without paying attention to the many issues that try to separate you from God's presence. Be it the self-serving disobedience of Adam and Eve that cost them their unique relationship or the years long struggle to overcome all the opposition that thwarted Joseph, including several compromises that are so prevalent in western society in our day. Maybe like David, we have sinned grievously and publicly and need to find the contrition and repentance that precedes a fresh start. We could, of course, be in one of the most dangerous seasons of life. It tastes so sweet, we call it success. Depression and emotional emptiness are sometimes also on the street called success, so we must be especially alert in the good times.

But I am hugely comforted that Jesus, the Son of God, was tempted in all points like we are, yet without sin; that He offers a shining example of how, in His strength, we can follow (sometimes falteringly) in His footsteps, knowing that, as with His friend Peter, He prays for us. He wants a relationship with us more than we do with

Him. Or, as expressed by the late Cardinal Basil Hume, "Our search for God is only our response to His search for us." Let us be vigilant and aware of the devil's schemes that try to break our communion and understand as, Hume continues, that "[Jesus] knocks at our door, but for many people their lives are too preoccupied for them to be able to hear."

The first category of challenges then are the *watch-outs*, the stumbling blocks, the side-tracks and the *"sin that so easily besets us."* There are other challenges to recognise. God is not restless, but He is always on the move. If we want to know Him more nearly and cherish His presence more dearly, we must "keep up".

In the story of the children of Israel entering the promised land by crossing the Jordan, the text says *"When you **see** the ark of the covenant..."* (Joshua 3:3). The ability to "see" the right thing was and is important. We must train ourselves in seeing well, improve our ability to identify the right things and better interpret what we see.

In the crossing over story the people were called to recognise God's presence and follow it, keep their eyes fixed on what He had promised (a new land) and trust Him and His ability to fulfil that promise. They needed faith because the practical out-working was, at least, bizarre, unusual and unique. In this sort of circumstance, to "keep up" is not always easy.

I have sat with many a tired preacher, weary on the journey, finding it a challenge to keep up. One, I remember, I had known from my youth. A faithful, disciplined and consistent man who had applied himself diligently to both his pastoral task and his academic

Remember the promises of God (handwritten margin note)

development. He was much older now, seemed a bit lost, unusually unfocussed and yes, he was very weary. I felt strongly prompted by the Holy Spirit to ask him, "What did the Lord say to you and promise you when you became a Christian those many years ago?" His eyes soon filled with tears and then he recited the words of some Scripture verses to me. "I haven't thought about those verses for years," he said. That was precisely why he was lost and weary. He had lost sight of God's promises to him and become lost in the jungle. He reminded me a long time later what a difference that moment had made. He saw again the promise of God, we prayed, he renewed his commitment and guess what? New energy and direction flowed into him.

Now, as I write, I am in another country. The steak is good; we've eaten in this restaurant before and the food is always enjoyable. I am delighted to be with a noble man who I respect. He is humble and godly and has worked long and hard in serving the Lord Jesus. He is, however, unusually down – not the vibrant man of faith I know. Life has struck some heavy blows over a number of years: sickness in his family, challenges (thankfully overcome) in the development of his children and death has come too close too soon. He is not impressed with the charismatic confessions of contemporaries who did not seem to stand the test of fire when death prevailed.

"It is allowed, you can doubt," I said. "In fact, where is true faith without doubt?" Yes, I know the Bible says, *"If we have faith and doubt not..."*. That is an unwavering and unshakeable confidence in who God is, what He has promised and His ability to do the impossible. We "doubt not" God's character. But there are unanswered questions, things we don't know – *"for the hidden things belong to God"* (Deuteronomy 29:29) – and yes, sometimes we can become weary in the "good fight of faith". It was a privilege to listen and hold my friend's hands up in his test, to remind him of God's promises to him, to speak encouragement and pray. He too needed to "see" again, gain a new perspective and take strength for the next leg of his journey.

Have you ever seen someone riding a bicycle with a dog on a lead, running alongside? If the speed is appropriate the dog can keep up, but if the cyclist gets carried away, then especially a smaller dog will try to run faster than it's legs will carry it! It may seem like that on our walk of faith – we are going faster than is comfortable. But be assured, *"He knows the way that you take…."* and will not go too fast or push you too far. Trust Him. I have often been comforted by The Message translation of the compelling words of Jesus in Matthew 11:28-30:

"Are you tired? Worn out? Burned out on religion? Come to me. Get away with me and you'll recover your life. I'll show you how to take a real rest. Walk with me and work with me – watch how I do it. Learn the unforced rhythms of grace. I won't lay anything heavy or ill fitting on you. Keep company with me and you'll learn to live freely and lightly."

In order to help us keep up, let us ask God to help us see and understand the beauty of walking with Jesus as we have just rehearsed. We need to keep in mind what God has promised, meditate consistently on His word and receive His strength. Then keeping up will, in His good time, bring us to our promised land and let us enjoy His continuing presence in a more profound, yet real way.

Before finally leaving the challenges we face in enjoying God's presence, one final reflection. There are many personality and gift assessment programmes that are designed to help us discover who we are, our strengths and weaknesses, and what we should be good at accomplishing. Without going into any of these systems allow me an over-simplification. Among many varied traits there are *adventurous* and *anxious* people. The adventurous can act before they think and the anxious can think so much that they forget to act. So, wherever we place ourselves along the adventurous/ anxious spectrum, God has a message for each of us: *it is time to "break out and advance"*.

Some people are naturally excited about new places, going where they have never been before, whilst others are more cautious and tentative. I could evaluate each of these traits, but do I need to? Most people know themselves enough to judge were they stand and know whether their challenge is that, "I'm too careless" or "I'm too cautious!" The book title is "Presence Carriers"; the passion of my writing is to encourage our spiritual thirst for more of the presence of God, whatever our natural disposition. So whilst we could beneficially reflect on the lessons of life learned and needing to be learned, (because we are too adventurous or not adventurous enough), I will limit my observations to a few specifics. I trust that as you are prompted and/or provoked to reflect more widely on other important issues, you will take the time to reflect, listen, and take advice in order to move forward to a better natural and spiritual place because you have been honest enough to stop, think and change.

It would appear that the centurion who appears in the story in Matthew 8 was more of an adventurer. He makes a humble but bold journey to speak with Jesus and expresses a profound understanding of authority as he invites Jesus to, *"just speak the word."* The story ends with Jesus saying, *"Go it will be done just as you believed it would"* (Matthew 8:13).

Even though he was bold and adventurous he needed a fresh injection of faith through Jesus speaking the word. It is the same for us. He was invited to go where he had never been before; to go and believe. He had to leave Jesus, confident that as he went home, a miracle had happened or was happening. He had to make that step of faith. The Bible concludes that his servant was healed at that very hour. The adventurous among us cannot achieve and accomplish everything simply by our boldness and "derring-do". An "I can do it", "get up and go" mentality has many advantages and rewards, but it will not part the Jordan or heal the servant or do what only God can do. That needs a word from God. So before rushing off adventurer, stop long enough to hear His word. This is maybe the missing part you need. You can then take whatever steps are necessary into the unknown with added confidence, knowing that He is with you, has gone before you, and has given you His word.

If that is Mr Adventurous what about Mr Anxious? In the opening story of this book, Max Lucado paints the picture of someone lost in the jungle. Later I referred to another of his jungle stories – of the man in deep jungle who, in his frustration, demands to know of his guide, "Where are we? Where is the path?" You may recall that the guide responded, "I am the path." It bears repeating here because we need to remind ourselves frequently that Jesus gives us Himself. To the over-cautious, those prone to anxiety, nervous about big decision making and unexcited about anything new or different: please hold His hand afresh. He knows the way; He has been here before; you can trust Him with everything. He is giving you Himself. He wants you to reach your promised land, but it will mean going where you have never been. Remember you have a gilt-edged promise: *"You will know which way to go."* But in order to discover the way, you must first set out! He promises He will, *"never leave you or forsake you"*, but you need to actively hold His hand and know His presence.

In the place of prayer and intimacy, it may mean for some who are more confessional and perhaps active "tongues speakers" that your journey is to a place of stillness and silence before the Lord. It may require more listening and waiting on Him ... with Him ... for Him. I promise you, it is worth it, although it will be quite uncomfortable to begin with. Maybe you are a Christ-follower who loves the Scriptures, who knows a quiet place of communion, but (and what a big "but" for you), the charismatic dimension of faith, the fullness of the Holy Spirit, is too much for you.

Let me urge you in the place of prayer to hear Jesus say to you, *"I will send you another Comforter"* and welcome Holy Spirit. Let Him have His way more fully in your life. Don't be put off by the unfortunate excesses of some who seem to produce no fruit of a Spirit-filled life. As David Watson, the renewed Anglican priest often said, "The answer to misuse is not disuse but right use." He was speaking of our attitude and approach to the work of Holy Spirit. For you, the journey may well at first be uncomfortable, but take a step of faith anyway. It will be worth it. You too will enjoy a greater experience of God's presence in you and with you. So let us all, whatever our natural and spiritual disposition, "break out and advance".

In conclusion, if you are a bit lost, even crushed or oppressed, seek afresh the presence of God. Get with some presence carriers. Keep obeying God's voice. He is the way and you will find the path to a better place.

If you need to see more clearly, maybe you need to stand still for longer. You will see more when you stop longer. You will hear more when you stop and listen longer. Then you will be ready to cross over, see and do new things, break out and advance.

All of us should make it our business to spend time formally and informally with other presence carriers. As we develop "spiritual friendships" we can more easily possess our promised land. Having heard His word it will have released faith in you, so maybe it is time for a step into the unknown. You will have a good story to tell! And finally, in the enduring advice of Proverbs 3, we are encouraged to acknowledge Him in all our ways. When we do, we can be sure that, as promised, He will make our paths straight (Proverbs 3:5-6).

It is time to leave our reflections on the challenges a presence-carrying life involves; time to turn our attention away from simply looking back and learning from ancient history. Now it is time to enjoy the dynamic positives that accompany the presence of God, which are most noticeable in the life of Jesus. But, please turn the page with care, for there is no one like Him!

Part Two

5
The Power of His Presence

It is one thing to recognise the presence of God in symbolism – pillars of fire and cloud are special – or parables, but God's protection and provision are more practical and of immediate use. As the pages of the Bible turn into the New Testament, something quite remarkably different happens. The people should have been prepared, but apart from one or two characters who were looking for "the consolation of Israel", the rest were walking in darkness. They had the witness of the prophets whose words were clear and unambiguous. For instance,

"But you, Bethlehem Ephrathah ... out of you will come for me one who will be ruler over Israel, whose origins are from of old, from ancient times." (Micah 5:2)

And Isaiah had said, *"Therefore the Lord himself will give you a sign: the virgin will be with child and give birth to a son, and will call him Immanuel"* (Isaiah 7:14).

Some of them knew where to find the information; they answered Herod's question about where the king was to be born with little difficulty; but they were not ready. The Jesus born to Mary did not match their idea of a Messiah. Most of them did not ever work out who He was and nothing much has changed. Immanuel, the Word made flesh, was God on earth. God had come to live in our world and down our street!

I have been thinking and speaking a lot recently about, "What happens when Jesus comes?" In this chapter we will explore some of the answers to that question. Jesus is the ultimate reality of God's presence with and in the human community. If it is true, and I believe it is, that He is the same yesterday, today and forever, then understanding what happened around Him in the Israel of yesteryear will inform our expectations of His presence with us now. So what did happen? Allow me some poetic licence as I think aloud!

* * *

It is hot. It usually is at this time of day. I am going for water. I've met some interesting people at the well over the months and years, but I tend to go there on my own. If the truth be told, most of the women don't like me. When they see me coming they look the other way, so I don't go early in the day when they all congregate together. Today I can see there is a man sitting on the huge stone that sits on top of the well. He looks like a Jew. That's strange, most of the Jews don't walk this route, they tend to avoid the road past Sychars well. I don't think anything "interesting" will happen today. As soon as I get near the well, he will probably get up and walk away so that we don't make any kind of connection...

Some time later...

Wow! Different? You can say that again! I've never come across anyone like him in my entire life. It's dark now and most of the village are asleep. I can't sleep yet, I'm too excited. That Jew that I saw, he actually spoke to me. He was disarming, vulnerable. He told me he needed a drink. What happened in the next few minutes is hard to explain. I don't think my life will ever be the same again. First of all, he treated me with such dignity – and men just aren't like that with me! Then he answered my questions. Not in the way I expected, but He made things so clear to me. He seemed to know all about my life. You would think that would be scary, but he was so kind and understanding.

There are so many things I could tell you about those brief moments we spent together talking, but I know you are busy, so I will just say this and let you go. I thought at first he was simply a thirsty traveller, but I soon realised he was a Rabbi. In fact, more than a Rabbi. As he spoke it became very clear he was a prophet. Then, and this is harder to say, I realised that this was God's Messiah. Don't ask me how, I just *knew*. Now I feel washed, clean, as though I have been given a new start in life. Most of the village walked back to the well with me. It was ... no, *He was*, amazing! He and his friends are sleeping in the village. I can't imagine what is going to happen tomorrow.

The unnamed woman of Samaria met Jesus and everything changed. Last Sunday among a number of people who were baptised in water was Jane. Life had closed in on Jane. She had family trouble, financial problems and had hardly left her house in the last two years except for hospital visits. Pills and more pills. She was very low. A wonderful Christian lady, Carol, introduced her to Jesus and the transformation was and is remarkable. Jane and the unnamed Samaritan – two women separated by 2,000 years of history, both met Jesus, who touched their lives and gave them the water of life to drink.

In the John chapter 4 story of the well, we see that Jesus breaks through so many barriers, including gender, religion and race. This woman was probably the first woman evangelist of the gospel age – rushing off to share how Jesus had transformed her life. He took her beyond a book, a place, tradition, herself, her past and much more. He will do the same today.

Let's think about another story. This comes much later in the life of Jesus on earth. Most commentators think they were probably a couple who had been married some years. Like many people they had hopes that life was about to get better. Specifically, they would have liked to see a change of government that would topple the rotten Romans from power. They had been utterly inspired by a young Rabbi who had given amazing talks, done unusual, even "supernatural" things – like healing the blind and raising dead people back to life. He was attracting quite a following and the power-brokers of the day, both the political and religious kind, did not like it one bit. So, last week they had hatched a plan, and like many other revolutionaries before him, now he was gone; dead and buried. Now the couple speak:

We thought everything was going to turn out so differently! We stayed in Jerusalem for a few days, but then what was the point? So we began to walk back home. We knew that if we kept going we should be there before night fall. The truth is though, we were not walking that quickly. We felt despondent, let down, disappointed. We had hoped for something better. So what now? Hopes dashed, we planned to return home and try to forget all about it. Tomorrow was another day.

But then we met a stranger on the road, who politely asked if we minded him walking with us. Honestly, we were glad of the company. It would keep our minds occupied. We concluded that he must be a traveller – he didn't seem aware of what had happened in the city over the last week. We talked about the usual things and then he asked us a strange question: "What were you discussing as you walked along?" We stopped, just stood there long faced. He didn't seem to know what had happened to Jesus of Nazareth. We confessed we had hoped he was "the one" – the one who would deliver Israel! But now he is dead – three days to the day. We told our mystery man a few more details, like not being able to find Jesus' body which had "gone missing" and about the rumours that were going around that he was alive. Never mind, we said, it was good while it lasted.

What happened next was amazing. He sounded a bit rude at first, asking why couldn't we "just believe". Then he explained to us the meaning of text after text, passage after passage of our holy Scriptures. He was still talking when we reached our village. We had walked about 7 miles. He took some persuading, but eventually he agreed to come and have some supper with us. What happened next is hard to explain. When the food was ready, we invited him, as our guest, to break the bread first. He said a blessing, broke the bread and shared it with us. In a flash – like a lamp being lit in a darkened room – both of us knew who he was – the living, resurrected Jesus! How? I'm not sure. Did I see the wounds in his hands? It was as if scales fell from our eyes and we just knew. We looked at each other in amazement, but in that split second, when we looked back at him, he had vanished ... gone. Adrenalin coursed through our veins and our hearts were on fire, remembering all he had said. It was unforgettable! We rushed back to the city, found the disciples and told them what we have told you. We will be telling everyone we meet. Life will never be the same.

* * *

Last week I met a man who was born into a Muslim family in West Africa and while training to be a doctor met many Christians. He had been asking his Iman why was it that God (Allah) did not speak to him? "I want God to speak to me," he said. His Christian friends had invited him many times to attend services, but he had never gone with them. One evening he felt strangely prompted that he should go to an all night prayer meeting that he knew his friends were attending. His own confession is that, "In the first Christian meeting I ever attended, I heard God speak to me. I asked God to forgive me and repented of my sins. I knew I was forgiven. What happened next, I later found out, was that I was filled with God's Holy Spirit." He has been a fervent Christ-follower ever since.

Once again, as in our earlier stories, the couple who found new hope on the Emmaus road and my African friend may be separated by 2,000 years, but they met the living Lord Jesus. He gave them new hope and perspective. His presence makes all the difference. So may I suggest that the first answer to the question, "What happens when Jesus comes?" is that people find new hope, purpose and direction in life. They are changed by meeting Him. They know the freedom that comes with forgiveness, their lives are transformed and their dreams are revived. Near the end of John's gospel he writes, *"Jesus did many other miraculous signs in the presence of His disciples, which are not recorded in this book. But these are written that you may believe that Jesus is the Christ, the Son of God and that by believing you may have life in his name."*

If you have never encountered Jesus, there is a promise here. He wants you to know and believe He is the Christ – God's anointed one and the Son of God, God walking in our world – and that in believing in Him you may know a different quality of life than anything else can offer you. He promises that all who seek Him will find Him. So, if you don't know Him, invite Him to make Himself real to you. If you do know Him, come to an even greater understanding of who He is and enter another level of knowing that, *"It is no longer I who live, but Christ who lives in me"* (Galatians 2:20)

The text I quoted also speaks about miracles, many not recorded in the written history of Jesus' time on earth. Thankfully, some are. This is the next thing that happens when He comes. They include *miracles of healings*: blind eyes seeing, the paralysed walking; *miracles in nature*: calamity and storm, turning water into wine; and also a number of incidents of *transformed lives by the casting out of demons*, including the story of an uncontrolled and uncontrollable man who was a danger to himself and his community. I love the narrative of this story. Picture it with me, this formerly wild, dangerous, "mad man", sitting there, dressed and in his right mind (Mark 5:15).

For the man helped by Jesus, this was the best day of his life. Sadly, for most of the community around him, what happened made them afraid, so they pleaded with Jesus to leave. Let us not do that. Yes, there are difficult questions, why some are healed and others are not. Yes, there is sometimes unnecessary and bizarre behaviour that accompanies the casting out of demons. But, please don't be overcome with fear, worried about the unusual, nervous that we are not in control of everything that happens. Rather, see those who are "dressed and in their right mind", no longer addicted, afflicted, sick or in pain; no longer living without hope and in despair.

For me, after decades of Christian service, I rejoice over the "little" miracles. For example, a lady coming to the front of a recent service, during our singing, saying that lumps that the doctors were monitoring in her hand had disappeared as we worshipped God. I can testify to warts vanishing in a service on my own hand when I was a very young boy. The "bigger" miracles – when x-rays show a different result than expected and life-threatening diseases "disappear" after prayer – all bring glory to God.

As a teenager I remember travelling to Spain with my family to meet a young English missionary. The roads were terrible, the sun was hotter than we thought and brought the expected consequences – sunburn! The police were terrifying, watching us closely as we bathed in the sea – all because in Franco's Spain people like us were perceived as dangerous and watched with suspicion. I only realised this week, while reading the recently published autobiography of Albert Garner, that the young missionary we visited had experienced a miraculous healing.

"Chris Rice felt strangely that God was calling her to missionary work in Spain. The doctor informed her that she had a tubercular lung and would not be allowed to leave the country. In desperation she knelt by her bed that night and pleaded with God for healing. After a short period of time praying, the same night she felt a warm glow within her body and knew without doubt that God had healed her. The same week, during an examination with her doctor, he confirmed her healing. As the amazed doctor then faced Chris, she gave testimony of how she was saved by Jesus and how by her bedside, after prayer, she was healed."[6]

Reading her testimony adds a glow to my memory of that time and powerfully underlines the point that there is power in His presence.

The ultimate "biggy" on the miracle scale is *resurrection*. The gospels tell several stories about it, including a son, a daughter and the more famous Lazarus, at whose tomb Jesus wept. The raising of Lazarus was the final straw for the powerless religious leaders. Their verdict was, "What are we accomplishing?" Then they concluded, *"Here is a man performing many miraculous signs. If we let Him go on like this, everyone will believe in Him, and then the Romans will come and take away both our place and our nation"* (John 11:47-48). Self-interest rather than meeting people's needs is a hallmark of this powerless "religious class" or, as the New Testament puts it, *"having a form of godliness but denying its power"* (2 Timothy 3:5).

All presence-carriers should maintain a confidence that the God of miracles is active and able to do anything! Yes anything! "For nothing is too hard for the Lord" (Jeremiah 32:17) and without the histrionics of some "charismatic agents", we can believe to see God's power manifest today, for His greater glory.

To understand the challenging words of Jesus, that we, His followers, should do greater things than He (John 14:12), must mean that we should expect to see lives transformed, dreams revived and miracles of many kinds accompany the preaching and living out of the gospel of Jesus. Alongside Christ's transformational work we can observe in His earthly ministry a kindness and compassion that breaks barriers of tradition, gender, race, religion and prejudice. It must be no different today. Whether it was the hated tax-collector, the unloved foreigner or the adulterous woman, Jesus reached beyond real and imaginary boundaries to touch need with His love and acceptance.

We must do the same! It is fascinating to notice that Jesus was "fully present" with each individual. For instance, the wise, respected Nicodemus, and the disrespected woman at the well – both of whose questions Jesus answers. The deeply troubled "legion", whose identity was wrapped up in his demon possession, also encountered Jesus' power, favour and kindness. In meeting each person's unique needs, yes Jesus brought wholeness, but also we see a strategy to touch wider constituencies. A voice in the camp of the Pharisees, a "revival" for the estranged Samaritans, and a gospel breakthrough in the unloved region of Decapolis where *"all the people were amazed"* (Mark 5:20). We too should believe that those with influence will meet and find Jesus through us and be catalysts for transformation in their community, in our time, the world over.

I have just returned from Ethiopia where I heard the most amazing first hand accounts of lives changed by encountering Jesus. One story was told of Jesus appearing during Friday prayers and thousands of people saw Him. He spoke to the leader saying,

"I have appeared to tell you that you are leading these people from darkness to darkness and from death to death. I will show you how to lead them to light and life." Many thousands of men and women have come to a living faith in Jesus Christ, in spite of difficulty and persecution. Individuals have had their wives and children taken from them, but having met Jesus they are determined to be His followers, whatever the cost.

We could explore many other facets, but this is merely a snapshot of what happens when Jesus comes. It is by no means exhaustive – either of the Bible history of yesteryear, the Church in the world today, or my own life experience of watching with wonder how Jesus, heals, helps and makes people whole. What is our response to this reflection on the unique realities of life when Jesus is present? For me, it produces an urgency to know Him more and consciously carry His presence into every moment of my life; for the wider Church, hundreds of millions of Christ-followers the world over, to be filled with a new enthusiasm and expectation that with Him present, anything and everything can happen. Whole communities can know transformation and we can witness in no small measure the coming of His kingdom and His will being done on earth. Your reaction to these ideas I must leave with you. I do, however, pray that deep within you is a hunger and a thirst to more consciously carry the presence of Jesus and see what He will do through you to His eternal praise and glory.

One final thought before we leave these reflections. I want joyfully to remind myself and you that the stranger who walked the road to Emmaus is the risen Jesus. He was no ghost or apparition. The resurrection power that brought Jesus out of the grave was of an altogether different magnitude than the Lazarus miracle. He, Jesus, lives by the power of an endless life. He, Jesus, has conquered death – it has no hold on Him. God raised Him from the dead. He is alive forever. All that He promised, He is overseeing. All God's promises are YES in Jesus. He longs to live in and through us by the working of Holy Spirit's power. May it be said of us when people leave our company, "I met Christ in a man today" or "I saw Jesus in the woman I met this morning" – and may God do something so amazing among us and through us, that the only person who can receive the credit and the glory is God Himself.

6
Shaped By His Presence

It has been well said that you can teach people what you know, but that you reproduce who and what you are. If this is true and we want to see ourselves with a secure identity, we should look no further than Jesus as our role model. His security and confidence in who He was, is wonderfully exampled in the story of Him washing the disciples feet (John 13). When He sat down after His "servant work", before explaining to them what He had done in setting them an example, He said, *"You call me 'teacher' and 'Lord', and rightly so, for that is what I am"* (John 13:13). He knew who He was and what He was about.

The story opens with plain statements about what Jesus knew about His identity: *"...that the Father had put all things under his power..."* (v3), *"...that he had come from God and was returning to*

God" (v3). So Jesus knew who He was, where He had come from, what He was doing, His authority for His work, the right timing of His actions, and where He was going. In such a secure understanding of His identity He shows His disciples "the full extent of His love", which includes doing the work of a slave.

It is critically important in knowing who we are that we understand the biblical principle that we are not fully human – in other words, we do not truly know who we are – until we find a personal relationship with God through Jesus Christ. Our knowing Him helps us to "know" ourselves and then we can "know" others. Bernard of Clairvaux, a Cistercian monk, in his profound book *Loving God* describes four degrees of love:[7]

1. Loving ourselves for our own sake
2. Loving God for His gifts and blessings
3. Loving God for Himself alone
4. Loving ourselves for the sake of God

The highest degree of love, for Bernard, was simply that we love ourselves as God loves us – in the same degree, in the same manner, and with the very same love. We love the self that God loves, the essential image and likeness of God in us that has been damaged by our sin. It is only when we allow ourselves to be shaped by His presence like this that we find our true identity. How many people have I met, old and young, strong and weak who, alongside the damage of sin in their nature and the hurts and harm of negative experiences, continue to be less than God created them to be because they refuse to believe how much God loves them, cares for them and has provided everything they need to become the man or woman of His original design. I hasten to add, it is an incremental work. We are changed from glory to glory. It works as an exchange. We give Him, in the words of Isaiah, our ashes, our mourning and our spirit of despair and He gives us a crown of beauty, the oil of gladness and a garment of praise. That is an exchange worth investigating.

As a boy I listened to very sincere people, not always with the best voices, sing out their understanding of what I am describing. They often used hymns. The first verse of one I remember being sung often speaks about life being "all of self and none of thee." Working its way through the stages of "the death of self" to the finale:

Higher than the highest heaven
Deeper than the deepest sea
Lord, thy love at last has conquered
None of self, and all of thee

An old friend of mine described it in a different, more abrupt manner. When we were in the company of Christians who were still full of themselves in all the ways that such carnality can express itself, my friend said to me, "Spiritual B.O. David!" In other words, the unpleasant smell of carnality or "spiritual body odour". How different to sit with someone, I'm thinking of two different Peggy's as I write, who have walked with Jesus a long way for a long time and who treasure His presence. They give off an altogether different "spiritual fragrance" – a perfume you are happy to enjoy. They are like Him. They have been shaped by being with Him and they live to please Him.

They say the longer you are with someone, the more likely it is that you will become like them. This is especially true of married couples who have shared a long life together. Maybe it is also true of the Bride of Christ, so that the more we are with Him the more we want to be like Him. I know the opposite is also true. When love is low and hearts are cold and our walk with the Lord Jesus is distant and indifferent, then our attitudes are harder, our compassion less sensitised. We are less like our Lord. We should therefore guard against anything that takes us away from Him.

The story of Jesus cleaning out the temple (Mark 11:15-17) by driving out the money changers and the cheating tradesmen, illustrates this point and brings a deeper meaning than my youthful understanding of being conscious of mixing business with worship. Peter Scazzero expresses it well: "Jesus' intense anger ... ought to make us gasp. He knows that if we don't get to God, invaluable treasures will be lost or obscured. We lose the space where we experience God's unfailing love and incredible forgiveness. We lose an eternal perspective on what is important and what is not. We lose compassion. We gain the world but lose our souls (Mark 8:36-37)." *So what is it that is cluttering the path to the presence of God for you?* Scazzero quotes Jean Danielou:

> "I have a need
> of such a clearance
> as the Saviour effected in the temple of Jerusalem
> a riddance of clutter
> of what is secondary
> that blocks the way
> to the all important central emptiness
> which is filled
> with the presence of God alone."[8]

So whatever it is, including the busyness of our Christian service, our fears or failures and our successes and substitutes, if it has blocked our path to enjoying more of God's presence, pray for a "clearance".

As we think and reflect on our identity and how we are shaped by His presence, I am drawn to remind myself that the issue of our spiritual transformation is not a casual matter. It will not just happen by chance and therefore requires intentional decisions, thinking and discipline to bring it about. We live in a world obsessed with charisma, "star quality" and celebrity, and too often the Christian community is swept along with the spirit of the age and forgets or neglects to speak about and model, the strong Bible truth that character is an essential foundation of our spiritual formation. God is more interested in who you are becoming than in what you do.

I have spoken around the world from Isaiah 49 using the phrase, *"He made me into a polished arrow"* (v2). I speak about the component parts of the arrow in order to illustrate the character development process. The pointed head reminds us of a person's gifts – the charis or natural/spiritual abilities implanted in us by God. The arrowhead represents the effective impact we have in life when we make a contribution using those gifts. The flights, often feathers, that guide the arrow to its target make me think of our much needed sensitivity to the Holy Spirit's direction and prompting and also the need to learn how to understand and work with people – the skill of getting along and working together. It is a long held observation that many people make every part of their lives more difficult, simply because they don't understand people and have not even thought about loving their neighbour as themselves! I believe this problem accounts for much of the discord in society, including churches.

The final part of the arrow is the shaft connecting the arrowhead and the flights. In ancient times, light tree branches were stripped of twigs and bark then soaked in water and pinned to the ground after being forced straight. Then they were left through day and night, so as to be subject in turn to heat and cold, for as long as it took to change their "character" – to make them perfectly straight.

God desires to form our character in much the same way, in order to provide the needed stability between our gifts and our awareness of the Holy Spirit's prompting. The character formation process is painful and life long, but of immense value. Think of the delight when our Lord and Master is able to take a fully prepared arrow and hit its intended "target", fulfilling His purpose. It is a pretty special feeling. Practicing the presence of God, having a listening ear for both encouragement and correction, being easily entreated and teachable, will all aid this process and render us fit for the Master's use. It is a vital part of our spiritual formation.

I will leave you to reflect on how you believe you are progressing. Maybe the blueprint of some of the Bible's significant characters will amplify what I have been saying. Moses, as we saw in an earlier chapter, was marked by God as a special person when a baby. His "being pinned down" journey had highs (in Pharaoh's palace) and lows (running away as a murdering fugitive) before his life was defined by an encounter with God. He was quick to answer when God called his name, *"Moses, Moses!"* *"Here I am,"* he said. Very commendable and a great example for us to be attentive and responsive to God's call. It is, however, interesting that as soon as God began to spell out His plan and it became clear that it included Moses (*"I am sending you…"*), he was uncertain of his identity: *"Who am I, that I should go…"*

Think about Jacob. He pretended to be his brother, stole a birthright and then lived away from home for two decades. He wasn't true to who he was and it cost him a lot. Only when asked, *"What is your name?"* during his wrestling match (Genesis 32:22-32), did his life change. Why? Because he owned up to who he was: Jacob, the cheat, the schemer and deceiver. But God changed him and his name. Jacob could face the challenge of brother Esau now and enjoy his new found identity. It happened through an encounter with God. It will be the same for you and me.

Gideon was similar when addressed as a "mighty man", while doing "clandestine, fear-filled work". All through Scripture and in the testimony of every generation of Christ-followers, meeting God and living attentive to His presence has shaped our identities. It will be the same in this generation for you and me.

God uses the ordinary and unusual events of life to mould and reveal. Both our flaws and potential are brought to light in His presence. I was an opinionated and somewhat "bigoted" Pentecostal in the early years of Christian ministry. Some of my childhood was spent in Northern Ireland where there was little understanding or tolerance either politically or spiritually between the peoples of Ireland. Much later I found myself invited to a Christian monastery with two older Pentecostal pastors. We shared afternoon tea with a group of about fifteen monks, then someone suggested we spend some time in prayer together. One of the monks began playing the piano and we sang The Lord's Prayer, after which the monks began singing "in tongues" with devotion, confidence and joy. Jesus was truly present by the power of the Holy Spirit and I had a rude awakening and wrestled with my many thoughts. I have had numerous experiences around the world that have, I believe, made me a better man and drawn me closer to God and given me a greater love for others. Do I still hold clear beliefs about many vital spiritual issues? Yes I do. But I know I have been shaped by His presence both directly and by meeting Him in His people, sometimes in the most surprising ways and places.

I read recently Kenneth E Bailey's book on Luke 15, *The Cross and the Prodigal*, and was deeply moved by his teachings of the stories about the lost sheep, lost coin and the lost son. I will draw only two of many wonderful points from the book to aid our reflection on how our lives are shaped. Western art shows the good shepherd with his staff in hand, well manicured hands and neat clothes and a sweet little lamb tucked under his arm. Bailey points out that the reality in the time of Jesus was almost certainly very different. It was tough terrain and difficult work. When the shepherd finally found his lost sheep, often injured, he still had much work to do before the party, where he could say, "Rejoice with me, I have found the sheep." He would tie its feet together and then carry the sheep of significant size and weight on his shoulders. It was tiring work. Have you ever thought how much work Jesus has done in providing our salvation on the cross and the ongoing work of carrying us home to the Father's house?

The prodigal son is even more dramatic. He knew he would be finished, the moment he reached his home village. As soon as the villagers discovered that his inheritance money had been lost among the Gentiles, the *Kezazah*[9] ceremony would be enacted and the people would disown him. His father disgraced himself, showing his legs and racing to the edge of the village to meet his disgraced and disgraceful, smelly and bedraggled son. Was the boy repentant? Probably not yet – he was hungry. He begins his speech, but not before his father, out of breath and filled with compassion for him, had thrown his arms around the boy and kissed and kissed and, yes, kissed again this scoundrel son. Bailey writes,

"How will the prodigal respond to this outpouring of costly love? 'And the son said to him, *"Father, I have sinned against heaven and before you; I am no longer worthy to be called your son."'* (v21)

Stunned beyond belief, the prodigal changes his mind and does not finish his speech! The offer to become a craftsman is deliberately set aside. He does not presume to offer any solution to their estrangement! Rather, overwhelmed, he can only put himself completely at the mercy of his father and say, 'I am no longer worthy to be called your son.' His surrender to his father's will is complete. At the beginning of the story he insisted on unhampered control over his own life. Now he leaves his destiny entirely in his father's hands. He is overwhelmed by this unexpected outpouring of costly love. Words originally composed to manipulate are transformed into a speech of genuine repentance.

Traditional Western interpretation has said that the father interrupted the son and didn't give him a chance to finish his speech. Rather, faced with this incredible event he is flooded with the awareness that his real sin is not the lost money, but rather the wounded heart. The reality and enormity of his sin and the resulting intensity of his father's suffering overwhelm him. In a flash of awareness he now knows that there is nothing he can do to make up for what he has done. His proposed offer to work as a servant now seems blasphemous. He is not interrupted. He changes his mind and accepts being found. In this manner he fulfils the definition of repentance that Jesus sets forth in the parable of the lost sheep. Like the lost sheep, the prodigal now accepts to be found."[10]

Remember what we are thinking about here – how our lives are shaped by His presence. Jesus, in His matchless storytelling, is further revealing "the full extent His love" (*"God so loved the world that He gave..."* – John 3:16), our need to be found, and the joy and acceptance that follow.

As with us, as found, forgiven sinners, the prodigal son finds a new source for his security and identity. It is in his father's love, forgiveness and welcome home. However he had served his father before his dreadful departure for the big city, there is no doubt now that it is genuine love and service and not self-interest that provide the motivation for this forgiven man. It should be the same for us. Understanding the hideous, odious impact of our sin and rebellion on the heart of our Creator, Father God, the full extent of His sacrifice in saving us, and to embrace the full benefits of our restoration to the "rights" of sonship should leave no doubt as to how and why we serve God. Not for gain, but in gratitude that God's grace has reached us, found us and brought us home.

Forgiven people serve differently. It is no longer about performance, but it is energised by passion. Out of our failure and brokenness we become authentic humans, made complete by God's presence living with and in us. His impact on our lives has the same effect as the potter's hand on the moulded clay.

We become the carriers of the "image and likeness of God" – the very thing that makes us fully human, liberates all our gifts and realises His grand design; the "you" He planned before He made the world!

Before we leave this chapter, I need some honest reflection. Knowing what God in Christ has done for me, am I as grace-filled and grateful as I should be? If, as I write, I am more potently aware that His presence has dramatically changed me and the life I live, am I as alert to the many distractions that lessen His impact on me, and am I as concerned as I should be about those many moments when I am careless and inattentive to Him? How much of my agenda and my selfishness still bleed through the otherwise pure motives of how and why I live as I do?

Maybe you have your own questions and responses to the concepts and ideas presented in these pages. If so, don't wait too long before you identify the questions and give yourself enough time and honesty to end in a better place because you have had the courage to stop and re-evaluate.

If what I said earlier is true – that in knowing God we begin to know ourselves – what does that true self look like? While we are reflecting and reassessing I believe this is an area of much confusion, with lots of contaminated thinking and modelling, over-influenced by an age of attitude and self-realisation. Writing about this more than sixty years ago, the Trappist Monk, Thomas Merton said, "Many poets are not poets for the same reason that many religious men are not saints: they never succeed in being themselves. They never get round to being the particular poet or particular monk that they are intended to be by God!"[11]

In his book, *Finding Sanctuary*, Abbot Christopher Jamison from the TV series *The Monastery* comments, "People fail to be themselves because it is easier to be somebody else and because they can copy somebody else's success rather than risk their own failure. Working hard to copy somebody else is in the end not selfless, it is, in fact, selfish. There can be an intense egoism in following everybody else. People are in a hurry to magnify themselves by imitating what is popular and too lazy to think about anything better."[12]

He notices how busyness and the false self go together: "Hurry ruins saints as well as artists. They want quick success and they are in such haste to get it that they cannot take time to be true to themselves. And when the madness is upon them they argue that their very haste is a species of integrity."

"In essence, he accuses much that passes for being true to oneself as more imitation of other people's experience. The real task of being true to oneself is a slow and profound work. It is not a fixed way but involves search and change. And in the end, being true to oneself can only be achieved by listening to God. Keeping busy is a way of avoiding being true to oneself. Let that sink in for a moment and then step further into the sanctuary. Merton offers an insight which illuminates the whole sacred space that is opening up in front of us and sets an agenda for life: 'In order to become myself I must cease to be what I always thought I wanted to be.'"[13]

One more paragraph from Abbot Jamison:

"If your life is centred on yourself, on your own desires and ambitions, then asserting these desires and ambitions is the way you try to be true to yourself. So self-assertion becomes the only way of self expression. If you simply assert your own desires, you may have the illusion of being true to yourself. But in fact all your effort to make yourself more real and more yourself have the opposite effect, they create a more and more false self. This self assertion is false because it cuts you off from other people. If your own desires are your guide in life then you end up imposing yourself on other people and then start demanding their affection, which can only be given, not demanded. So asserting your own desires is the opposite of loving behaviour. As well as longing to be true to yourself, you long to love and be loved, which means that you must find a way that combines being true to yourself with love."[14]

Merton would pray, "Pray for your own discovery." The agenda of your life is set neither by other people nor by yourself; it is set by God. Life becomes the search for God's agenda in your life. When you find it, then you have found your true self. You have found the ultimate, obedient freedom.

If like me, your spiritual roots are in a very different spiritual tradition, you may dismiss the above as "too Catholic". You can either deflect it because it is too demanding or embrace it as I do because you long to be fully shaped by God's presence and fully *"conformed to the likeness of His Son"* (Romans 8:29). In so doing we can live as authentic human beings, living comfortably in our own skins without the hypocrisy of a false self, the cling film or veneer of a pseudo-spirituality and free to be "the slaves of Christ".

I finish the chapter with a written prayer I prayed today:

"Abba Father, I open my clenched fist to surrender everything you have given to me. Reestablish my identity in you – not in my family, my work, my accomplishment, or what others think of me. Cleanse the things in me that are not conformed to your will. By faith I invite my will to be yours so that the likeness of Jesus Christ may be formed in me. In His name. Amen."[15]

1
Directed By His Presence

Some of us may feel that it is an admission of weakness or failure to confess the need for direction. Others may feel comforted by the assurance of knowing and having a "guide". It is alarming to realise that at this simplest level, the wilderness people of Exodus only went where God's presence took them. Yet, even with such obvious direction from the cloud and pillar of fire, they were a generation late in arriving where He was leading them and often missed the best of God's plan for them.

At one level, the many "guidance" texts of the Bible are comfortable and comforting. At another level they demand a high level of trust and maybe they also keep us on our toes and more dependent than our "old nature" finds easy.

Who wouldn't enjoy the "balm" of verses like,

> *"I will guide you with my eye..."* (Psalm 32:8 NKJV)
> *"This is the way, walk in it..."* (Isaiah 30:21)
> *"Acknowledge Him in all your ways and He will direct your path [steps]..."* (Proverbs 3:6)
> *"Walk with me and work with me, watch how I do it..."* (Matthew 11:28-30 The Message)
> *"You will know which way to go, since you have never been this way before..."* (Joshua 3:4)

With this in mind, how do we ever go wrong? How do we miss the path? How do we end up in the wrong place at the wrong time?

I have watched with interest in some of the more difficult shipping lanes and the tricky harbour berths of the world, how very experienced sea captains trust and need the expertise of a pilot. Why would our life passage be any different?

Phil is a larger than life preacher friend in whose company I am always refreshed. He loves his family and delights to collect one of his grandsons from school some days each week. Zach is now six years old, but the story Phil told me happened before his last birthday.

"How did you get on at school today, Zach?" Phil asked.
"Okay, Poppa, it was a good day."
Silence.
"Do you want to know what really happened, Poppa?"
"Of course, son, Yes."
"Well, we had quiet reading today. That means that with two of

my friends, we can go into the corner of the classroom and read whatever books we choose."

"That sounds exciting, what did you read?"

"I asked my friends if they would like me to read them a story about Jesus from the Bible. They both thought that was a good idea."

So Zach read a story from the life of Jesus and asked his friends some questions and they talked about the story. He then asked his friends if they would like to know Jesus as their friend and they both said "Yes".

"Well," said Zach, "Then you need to pray a prayer like this..." and he proceeded to pray a "sinner's prayer" and asked them to pray it after him, which they did.

"That was brilliant Zach!" Phil exclaimed. "What was the prayer?"

"Oh, it was the prayer you pray Poppa, when you pray for people in church."

"That's very good."

More silence.

"Poppa, would you like to know what really happened?"

"Sure."

"Well, I laid my hands on their heads and prayed over them like you do. They thought it was all great."

More silence.

"Do you want to know what really happened today, Poppa? I think I had a spiritual breakthrough. I have wanted to pray with my friends for a long time."

"I think you did have a breakthrough, Zach."

More silence.

"I have been thinking one more thing Poppa. Do you want to know what it is?"

"Of course I do."

"I've been thinking ... what is your next big breakthrough, Poppa?"

Maybe for some of us our big breakthrough is learning how to be directed by His presence, or being more skilled in listening to the direction He gives us? Maybe our need is to realise how much we need His direction? Whatever it is, heed the words of a young boy and attend to the important issue of your next breakthrough.

Let us think about why we need direction. Yes, we can easily get lost and some of us are unhealthily independent, but I believe there are some deeper reasons. First, I believe we are created to connect with the divine. Part of being fully human is to enjoy "containing" and being "connected" to God, which carries with it the blessing of someone who is Alpha and Omega, who knows everything and is willing to share His wisdom with us lesser mortals. Then I believe we need direction to fully understand God's unique will and plan for our lives individually. We will never see enough of the picture left to ourselves. Thirdly, Paul speaks about a mystery which includes an eternal purpose, an intention and a manifestation of God's manifold wisdom through a named entity – the Church. We need divine direction to fully play our part in such a massive enterprise.

The Bible makes some very clear and unambiguous statements. Here are a few:

God the Father, *"...so loved the world that he gave His only begotten son..."* (John 3:16)

Jesus Christ, *"...loved the church and gave himself up for her..."* (Ephesians 5:25)

The gospel makes it very clear that the passion and desire of Holy Spirit is to make Jesus real and known to us. *"He will bring glory to me by taking from what is mine and making it known to you"* (John 16:14).

Let us think about these statements in the light of our involvement and place in His Church. Christ is the head of the Church. He is also its foundation, so we can't make progress in knowing our place in it without a growing love for and knowledge of our Saviour, Jesus. How will this happen? By a work of Holy Spirit. The more we know of His presence and power, the more He will reveal Jesus to us. Now, the more we know and enjoy the love and friendship of Jesus, the more we will love what He loves – and He loves the Church. Together they will help us find our place and use our gifts to empower our service. Jesus will also make His Father known to us. He says, *"I and my father are one ... anyone who has seen me has seen the father"* (John 10:30; John 14:9). In knowing and loving the father, we will also love what He loves and He loves the world! "World" here means cosmos, order, the arrangement of things.

Remember we are recognising our need to be directed by His presence, so how might what I have just described look like for each of us?

First, a dynamic, relevant and compelling enjoyment of God's Holy Spirit living in us and calling out of us a life of holiness and of making Jesus known to us.

Second, a lifelong adventure in a deepening love relationship with Jesus, who restores our souls and gives our lives an eternal and spiritual relevance that echoes with the deepest parts of our being.

Third, we find community, "our place", connectedness and belonging in a living entity called "the Church", because Jesus loves it and wants us involved in it; not as a religious structure, but as people joined together as "living stones" or "parts of a body", made fit for purpose and fulfilling what we were born to be and do.

Then fourth, we learn that life works best when we enjoy God's order, with everything in and around our lives arranged the way He wants it to be. Continuing chaos, which drains the life out of everything and everybody, is replaced by an order that far from limiting our lives, brings perfect freedom. There is much to be said about God's order, including His authority structures in our lives, homes, families, church, work and wider society. For example, fathered families provide a basic building block in society and the absence of such makes for many challenges. But I must not digress into this too far. Suffice to say, continuing and deepening levels of chaos in any and every part of life are a sign that the Father's "order" is not yet fully present. Finally on this point, our lives have greater focus, purpose and meaning as the "unforced rhythms of grace" that life in Christ opens to us bring "shalom", rest, and relaxation to the whole of our life and service. We find ourselves truly "hidden with Christ in God" (Colossians 3:3).

Now let us think about the nature of God's direction. His guidance is not a compensation for our inadequacy, but a necessary part of our relationship that is designed to release us into fullness. I mean a full cup, a fulfilled life, a place of appropriate satisfaction and contentment. There is no place for feeling we are inadequate because we need His help. Rather, part of our adequacy is knowing that we are designed to want and need His help. It is all part of the interdependence that makes us fully human.

Then, God's direction is not to rob us of choice or freeze our minds. We are not sat-navs waiting like a robot for a download of data. Campbell McAlpine made a relevant comment: "You will find in life there are very few crossroads of decision, but many milestones of obedience." The Bible promises to give us the desires of our hearts and invites us to "choose" who we will serve. God will provide all the information we need to make the next appropriate step, but the choice is ours. Maybe God's full information is "limited"? Could it be that He is developing a life of faith and trust in us, alongside our experience in making good choices? I heard someone else say recently, "If God's will does not intimidate you, what you are planning is probably an insult to Him."

We also need a revelation of how superior God's will is compared with ours. We can make our plans, but they are usually too mean and limited. We are wise to learn that His ways are higher than our ways, His plans better than our plans, His "sight" better than ours. We should choose the words of the Psalmist: *"I delight to do your will O my God"* (Psalm 40:8 NKJV). It is good to often remind ourselves of the promise of direction. Proverbs 3:5-6 teaches us to, *"In all thy ways acknowledge Him and He shall direct thy paths"* (KJV). Our responsibility is the continuing recognition of His presence and place in the "everything" of life, including how we spend our time, money and use our gifts. His very presence is direction. That truth is worth remembering every day.

I am reminded of a story about a godly Second World War solider who found himself in serious trouble because his commanding officer thought he was communicating and collaborating with the enemy. Yes, he was spending much time alone, but it was for the purpose of acknowledging the Lord in a serious commitment to prayer. His commanding officer did not believe him. In desperation he was commanded to pray in front of his superiors. The moment he prayed out, all present knew that what they heard was the outflow of a life of devotion and he was quickly stopped. His commitment as a spiritual soldier saved him in a tight situation. We must learn in everything to give thanks and acknowledge the Lord. His promise will be ours also.

I will end this chapter with a few reflections around the truth that our confidence is not misplaced when we believe that He who began a good work in us will carry it on to completion (Philippians 1:6). God is not only a starter, He is also a finisher. He is Alpha, yes, the beginning, and He is also Omega, the end. You could say, therefore, He only begins because He has already finished. From the opening of the Bible in creation God has been finishing His "work" and it is all good. It is His nature. He will not change. If, then, by His unexplained grace, you know that God has begun a work in your life, you can remain confident that He will not leave or abandon it. He will finish what He has begun.

What might that "finish" look like? A prospered life, answered prayer with natural and spiritual blessings? Maybe and probably, but these things are never His main work. He wants to conform you to the image of His Son. He wants you to be like Christ. He wants your and my life to reflect His "image and likeness". Nothing less will be sufficient. I have become aware over decades as a

Christ-follower, that no incident or experience, no pleasant or difficult event in our lives will ever be wasted in His determination to reach the goal of you being like Christ. So in the public and private parts of life, the so-called sacred and secular, the mundane and the exciting, He is always working. If we understand this, it is not important what happens to me, but how I react to what God already knows is happening to me.

So many people have not grasped this truth. They make wrong judgements about the many things that happen throughout life. The reactions are kaleidoscopic. *What have I done wrong? I'm being punished. Why me? I don't' deserve this. I am worth it – I do deserve this.* People react, fight, defend, complain, boast, myriad words and reactions, all the time missing the point that all of it, the good, the bad and the ugly, are like a hammer on the hot metal on an anvil, seeking to shape and conform our lives into something magnificent, eternally enduring; a work of art made like Christ.

The sooner we understand this principle the easier the process will be to "pass through". The longer we fight, run away, change jobs, partners, churches or whatever, the longer the process will continue. When we learn what we are being taught and change our character to become more like Him, the heat can subside, at least for a season. But never forget, if He has begun, He will finish. So the more malleable, pliable and flexible we are, the more His presence shapes and directs our lives and the easier the journey will be.

He promises to guide us with His eye. He knows where He is going, where the path is and what needs to happen. Trust Him. Be directed By His presence. It will be worth the journey.

Before you continue to the next chapter, are there any issues in this chapter that demand your attention and may need courageous action? Remember the little boy's challenge, "What's your next big breakthrough, Poppa?"

Well, what is yours?

8
Practicing His Presence

If we understand the major themes of the second part of this book as true, namely that His presence has power and will shape and direct our lives, then we need help and encouragement in "practicing His presence" and making it an integral and vital part of the rhythm of our lives. Inspirational models, best practice and a God-given hunger and thirst will give our journey impetus.

So often in life we are oblivious of the things around us, then someone points out a trend, a "thinking", something newly popular, and all of a sudden we begin to notice it everywhere. Living aware, being alert and attentive to the constancy of His presence is a helpful starting point. How do I live with my eyes open to the fact of God being present with me in every moment of life? That is what I mean by practicing His presence.

Canon Andrew White, known as "the Vicar of Baghdad", who recently visited the Christian Centre in Nottingham, sharing inspirational and challenging messages, says in his most recent book,

"When things are bad here in Baghdad it is always a temptation to allow oneself to spiral into despair or fear. During such times I am challenged to remain in God's presence. From the place of His presence I respond to circumstances very differently – not from an earthly, emotional perspective, but from a supernatural one. When I think about living in God's presence it means three specific things to me:

It is about living 'in His glory'.
It is about the presence and guidance of His Holy Spirit.
It is about the gifts that God gives us to accomplish His will on earth."[16]

He is being alert and attentive, co-operating with Holy Spirit and carrying God's presence with him everywhere.

Maybe we will be helped if we pay attention to the language we use when we talk to God in private and in public. I have heard people pray in a multitude of contexts. Some are speaking with a God they know is fully present. Others speak as though God is far away and uninformed about their situation. Still others are disrespectful – they would never speak, shout and perform the way they do in prayer if they were speaking to a fellow human being in the flesh, stood before them – so why do it to God? We don't need to extend an invitation to God to "come to our meetings" when we realise He is already present.

Someone who is "in love" becomes very aware of their lover – how near they are, how happy they appear, whether or not their needs are being attended to. Should we not cultivate a lifestyle of such heightened awareness around our lover, Jesus? Learning sensitivity, attentiveness, being fully present, simply enjoying being with Him? I am sure a more positive approach to holiness, expressed elsewhere in this book, would greatly help us in this quest. The primary emphasis of biblical consecration is to please God more than it is a departure from sin. Yes, holiness includes an element of "moving away from" – what we forsake, leave behind and refuse to engage in or think about. But it is very much more about "movement towards" – an active progression into enjoying God's company and understanding that involvement in that "other" life does not please Him or make Him comfortable in our company.

We need to help ourselves and those in our discipling circle to develop listening prayer. Let me repeat some ancient wisdom and ask you to reflect on where you believe you are in response.

Prayer usually begins with us *talking at God*. In other words, there is a very limited understanding of any relationship. Then, we *talk to God*. It is now more than just us sharing information or making requests and demands. It includes emotion, love, gratitude and thanksgiving. If we grasp this and move forward, then now we are ready for a conversation – *talking with God* – which includes learning to listen to and interpret His words, His emotions and capturing what is on His heart. As this prayerful journey continues, we reach another level of intimacy and closeness where our prayer is the framework of a bigger picture. This is simply *being with God*. There may be words, but there is often silence. In human love it is a smile, a touch, a look, a known gesture and, yes, some words.

If I am serious abut practicing His presence, I need to develop and move through these stages of prayer. You may use different language to describe the process. Different Christian traditions use and enjoy a variety of forms and styles. However you arrive there, keep in mind the goal: a close, intimate, conscious knowing of Him. Solomon described it this way: *"My lover is mine and I am His"* (Song of Solomon 2:16). Once enjoyed in any measure of fullness, life is forever incomplete without Him.

Natural temperament and spiritual tradition will place us in a particular place along the spectrum of how we practice the presence. At one end are those who are vocal and active in their expression. At the other, those who are more reflective or passive. This often reflects both the natural and spiritual behaviour of a person. We are all different and God celebrates our diversity. Sometimes, when I find myself worshipping with those who always tend towards quietness and reflectiveness in prayer, I want to say, "I wish you would also learn how to be enthusiastic and energetic in your prayer and worship." Then when I am with that active, noisy lot (I grew up with them!), I sometimes want to say, "Oh please, will everyone be quiet and still? I can't hear for the noise!" Finding the right balance and being comfortable in different places along the activity and noise spectrum is a skill I am still acquiring. How about you?

For centuries there has been debate, argument and disagreement about asceticism. Many pious traditions have involved self-flagellation and extreme privation – the hair shirts and spiked beds brigade! Such behaviour has angered many who see all such extreme actions as "works", emphasising human effort and minimising the grace of God. In expressing a need to cultivate discipline, I am not for a moment moving from an understanding of the gospel that Paul expressed as, *"by grace you have been saved, through faith – and this not from yourselves, it is the gift of God – not by works, so that no-one can boast"* (Ephesians 2:8-9).

I am conscious that many religious traditions use forms of asceticism that are seen to strengthen and help spiritual development or even as a means of salvation. I want to repeat and make very clear that I am not, in any way, advocating a works-based salvation. I am not promoting the extremes of some of the older Christian traditions in history. I understand Paul's teaching in 1 Timothy 4, where he strongly repudiates the imposition of unnecessary religious rules. I am also nervous that in reaction, most Protestant spirituality, especially the Pentecostal and Charismatic traditions, have a very frail understanding of appropriate spiritual disciplines that can greatly help us practice and enjoy more of the presence of God.

I have been helped by a simple understanding of *askesis* – a Greek Christian term for the practice of spiritual exercises. It helps us shy away from the heavy end of asceticism, but encourages a life of meaningful devotion that pulses to the rhythm of developed spiritual exercises. It is helpful to find the balance between intense, focused behaviour, like an extended water-only fast, and a rhythm that can be sustained on a permanent basis.

Each of us must learn what disciplines help us most in drawing nearer to God and living presence-filled lives. Some are brilliant at journaling and find it most helpful. I understand some of its value, but am not good at it and prefer to do other things. Early morning reading of the Bible and other helpful devotional books is food to my soul. As I have grown older, longer times of silence and sitting in God's company help me know Him better. I have mentioned elsewhere a list of the most respected disciplines and simply urge you to find what helps you most to practice His presence in a sustainable way in this season of your life. Do remember to be open to change and to realise that in the different stages of life, different disciplines may need to be learned and enjoyed.

I have also spoken earlier that learning how to trust in the Lord, to live in communion with Christ, will make being guided and directed constantly a dynamic possibility. I have spoken of alignment, which makes life easier, and how attending to and being conscious of the peace of God will help us immensely as presence carriers. There is work for us to do here if we are serious about being "carriers of God", but let us keep this work in its proper place and right perspective.

My friend, Van Shore, recently sent an email reminding me of a John Wimber phrase that helped my understanding of this right perspective. I quote his email:

"Over recent days, God has made me aware that the expression used by the late John Wimber, 'God showing up', is best understood when we see it from God's perspective – namely, He is always waiting for us to 'show up'! When we 'show up', it is then that He can give expression to His presence and glory in ways that will certainly eliminate any idea that it has been about us."

The ultimate presence carrier was Jesus. C.S. Lewis helps our understanding of Jesus in his inimitable style. In his classic book, *Mere Christianity,* he says, "Either Jesus was, and is, the Son of God or else He was insane or evil. But, let us not come up with any patronising nonsense about His being a great human teacher. He has not left that open to us, He did not intend to ... We are faced then with a frightening alternative ... However strange or terrifying or unlikely it may seem, I have to accept the view that He was and is God."

I agree, Jesus is God, who walked in our world in the flesh. Let us not, however, make the mistake that it was primarily His "God-ness" that revealed Father God to us. If that is exclusively true, we have no hope of being like Him. No, Paul teaches us that He voluntarily laid aside every advantage of being God:

"Christ Jesus: who, being in very nature God, did not consider equality with God something to be grasped, but made Himself nothing, taking the very nature of a servant, being made in human likeness, and being found in appearance as a man, He humbled Himself and became obedient to death – even death on a cross." (Philippians 2:5-8)

It follows that through His spiritual disciplines and a life filled with the Holy Spirit, He made God known to men. From His nights of prayer and daily communion with His Father, His constant listening, and a strong desire to please His father by only doing what He saw the Father do, and much more, He modelled for us a devoted and disciplined life that constantly carried the presence of God for all to see. It was demonstrated by kindness and compassion, amazing wisdom and revelation of truth – a continuing flow of miraculous happenings, leading to many people finding hope, help and happiness.

If we are to remotely succeed in following in His footsteps, we must seek to live as He did. How then, do I summarise the characteristics of Jesus' ministry and life on earth? He was flexible, able to change His approach as the need required. He listened constantly, always aware of His Father's voice. He joined in with what He saw God, His Father, was doing and He never allowed Himself to be encumbered by a particular methodology. All His actions were saturated in a holy, happy life of closeness to His Father, supported by persistent spiritual disciplines played out in a life of humble service as God kissed the world with love through His Son – the incomparable Jesus of Nazareth.

I believe many of our preconceived ideas of what Christian service looks like, lived out on a canvas of religious practice, hinder rather than help the dynamic expression of God's life in us. It is important that we engage and model what I have just described in Jesus – devotion and actions that breathe the life of God into every part of our lives, responding as God prompts and helps us. Like Jesus, living this way may mean "breaking" some taboos and ignoring some religious rulers. Jesus never allowed their "rules" to stop Him doing good and even healing on the Sabbath. As I leave this topic, I can hear the words of an old hymn playing in my head or heart! "To be like Jesus ... all I ask is to be like Him." I trust that captures your heart's response too!

I will reflect on one other perspective of enabling the practice of His presence before ending this chapter. There is much talk in the western world of the work/life balance. Numerous studies have been carried out and there are many "management" programmes designed to help people avoid burnout and breakdown in the hectic pursuit of wealth, happiness and a sustainable lifestyle.

"Mastering the obvious" has been a significant preoccupation of mine for some years. What do I mean by this? That so often in life, our greatest areas of blindness relate to the things which should be so obvious to us. For instance, from a Christian perspective, why do so many people ignore the injunction to take one day of rest each week and further periods of reflection and rest throughout the year? Why do so many rest from work without an understanding that life is to be lived working from rest? Why do so many forget that when God spoke over His finished creation, alongside the amazing statement that it was all "very good", He revealed that He had "finished His work". Why then do so many people live as though God is not in control, doesn't know what He is doing and has run out of ideas, therefore requiring our assistance?! We waste precious time and use up needless energy in worry, fretting and being preoccupied with things that God has already promised He is watching over and taking care of. All this inappropriately stresses us, unsettles our life-rhythm, militates against the presence of God's shalom and our awareness of His presence, and saps our energy and enthusiasm for life.

I am a Gentile, but let me give you a somewhat clumsy view of a different rhythm of life, as lived out in many Jewish families for thousands of years. In this rhythm, our 24-hour day is divided into four major components. Unlike our day, which starts in the morning, their day begins at sunset. The evening is spent with family and friends, enjoying food, friendship, fellowship and fun. This is followed by the second significant period consisting of rest and sleep. The third part, early morning, is reserved for devotion and reflection and the fine-tuning of the mind, emotions, spirit and body. Then, and only then, begins the part we call "work" – the running of businesses, making a living, acquiring an education.

In this *askesis*, every part of the human life and psyche is prepared for whatever stresses the day of work will bring. In devout households all this is lived out as a sacred trust in devotion to God as an act of love and gratitude for His provision and many blessings. Nothing is secular, not even work – all is sacred and holy. Just maybe, there are some parts of that way of life and practice we can learn from. I believe that as we do, we will be better informed on our spiritual journey and more consciously carry the presence of God – the net effect of which will be lives lived in greater rest and personal fulfilment, and all around us people will be helped and blessed as they meet the presence of Jesus in us and our actions. That truly is a win/win scenario.

Your body is a temple, created by God, specifically designed to carry His presence. We carry *"this treasure in jars of clay"* (2 Corinthians 4:7). As we learn the secrets of practicing His presence, the promise which accompanies the above scripture will be ours. Our lives will, *"show that this all surpassing power is from God and not from us."* As we "contain" the presence of God, so we reflect His glory. We are transformed into His likeness with ever increasing glory (2 Corinthians 3:18). Let's keep practicing!

9
Nurturing His Presence

If it is true that His presence shapes and directs our lives and that we are fully human when we are "full" of His presence and interdependent with others, then it is important to nurture a presence-carrying culture in our lives.

I believe we will be helped if we look at this in at least two ways. We will look at what is our personal responsibility – what can only I do to nurture His presence? But first, what of the wider contexts of our lives, especially the role and place of the Church?

The word "culture" is used to mean many things today. One of the simplest understandings of culture is "a place where something can grow and develop". With that thought in mind, is the culture of church – our church – and indeed any community experience we are committed to, helping or hindering our appetite and desire to be a presence carrier? Here are some honest, personal reflections.

There seems to be a lack of experiential knowledge of and hunger for God's presence, especially in much of the Western Church. Our gatherings often become trapped in traditions, more an expression of religion than relationship, or alternatively so casual and trivialised that they could be mistaken for many other forms of human community or association.

Some expressions are exceptionally well organised, are format-driven and programme-orientated, both in the content of the "services" and the structure of church life. Then, we are more influenced than we probably want to admit by the consumer culture of much of modern life. We may have a "fast food" style survival spirituality, that deals only with our short term cravings and does not provide long-term, healthy development. Or maybe ours is a spiritual "speed dating" that emphasises connection without covenant, commitment or community, leaving the deepest parts of our natural and spiritual life undernourished and often compromised.

Time is also a major issue. The journey to true love, intimacy and knowing takes time, whether it is in our homes with the various relationships that exist in a family – especially that of wife and husband – or in our hearts as we "discover God" and "uncover" ourselves in His special company. Nothing else can do what only time together can achieve. So the strictly timed service, the "let's get this over so we'll have the rest of the day free" spiritual fast food option will not provide a culture in which we can nurture what we are considering here.

Let me quickly add that hours-long services, focused or unfocused, won't necessarily be any more helpful to us. However and wherever we meet, our focus should be on "meeting Him, who our souls long for."

They tell me that the best way to teach bank tellers to recognise counterfeit currency is by getting them to consistently handle "real" money – the genuine article. Surely this principle applies to the spiritual dimension also. If a person hasn't encountered the genuine, then any substitute is thought to be the real thing. I am, however, strongly heartened that a generation is growing who are tired of a tepid spirituality and thirst for an authentic encounter with God, well aware that it will cost more than the easy thrills of a modern world, but "buy" more than we can ever imagine.

I am now on dangerous ground. Could I be setting myself up as some sort of specialist and expert in this field, making judgement on all and sundry? That is not my desire. I am still a learner, a seeker after truth. But after many years of observation of the Christian community around the world, I truly believe these comments and warnings are legitimate and maybe necessary.

How then should those of us actively involved in the Church respond? What needs renewal? What must change? What is permanent? What should finish or flourish? We owe the next generation of Christ-followers the honour of passing to them a Church where people can meet God, be changed by the gospel, learn how to love and know Him, and carry His presence to a dying, broken and God-needy world.

There are schools of thought that find it difficult to understand the necessity of "the Church" – both in its "gathered together" setting and its "scattered throughout a community" context. Yes, the Church is made up of "living stones" and each of us must develop a life of discipline and devotion that is personal and often private. We must have a unique responsibility for our walk with God and how we live out the picture language of Jesus. He said we are to be like "salt" – only effective when it is spread around to provide seasoning in the world around it. He also said we are the "light of the world", so wherever we go, the light should be greater and the darkness less.

But alongside our responsibility to exhibit Christ personally, as *"a letter read by all"*, we flourish in contexts where we know others and are also known by them – from family through friendship, geography, affinity and much more. In some appropriate way we should "do life together" and in doing it, be discipling and being discipled as a natural and deliberate consequence.

We need environments that intensify our longing and desire for God. There should be no competition between my "alone" experience, my smaller community experiences, and the times when I am part of a larger, gathered congregation of Christ-followers. Anyone who over-concentrates on any one of these, especially to the exclusion of the other two, is potentially robbing us of an appropriate "culture" in which our spiritual life can uniquely grow.

I have been in many leadership contexts where executive decision making and legal governance have swamped the discipleship agenda. I understand that in such settings what we are and how we think, speak and act and will have an impact either positively or negatively on those around us, but I am saying that so often the process lacks intentionality. Discipling becomes accidental, a by-product, rather than being a commitment to helping each other grow by holding each other accountable for our words and actions – encouraging the good and challenging the bad.

Our highest level of spiritual involvement should be our first level of discipleship, both in making disciples and being discipled. We develop relationships and a trust that provides an atmosphere, a culture, where vulnerability and openness help us to grow; where appropriate risk taking and new steps are encouraged and watched over and where "failure" is not a destination but a place of learning.

I was recently riveted by the words and behaviour of Jesus. I have been overwhelmed by Him and His actions many, many times in my life and I pray the experience will continue for the rest of my life. Why? Because He is such an amazing person and I want to be inspired and helped to be more like Him. My recent experience happened as I reflected on two passages in John's gospel.

First, Jesus confesses in John 5:30 that, *"By myself I can do nothing."* Then He says, *"I judge only as I hear."* Finally, He states, *"For I seek not to please myself but Him who sent me."* He is admitting His dependence on His Father, His need to listen and His desire to please. Why should it be any different for us lesser mortals than for the "Word made flesh"?

The other passage that took my attention was that of Jesus washing His disciples' feet recorded in John 13. I have expressed elsewhere in this book the context of confidence and security Jesus possessed in knowing who He was, where He had come from, what He was doing and where He was going (v1-3). The point that fascinated me, however, was His preparedness to undress, literally, in order to take the place of the serving slave in front of the young men He was discipling. He makes Himself vulnerable and terribly open to mis-judgement. Why, in the leadership settings I have often been in, is there so little dependence, such poor listening and such insecurity and lack of vulnerability?

In maturing a presence-carrying culture among leaders, I believe these are huge principles to grasp, implement and pursue in becoming more like Jesus. The right culture makes such a difference. If we can capture the right atmosphere among leaders as we serve together, than we can expect the right culture for those we lead, to help them grow and become all they were created to be.

Leaders need discernment to facilitate and not stifle emerging gifts. In small and larger gatherings we must cultivate an environment that gives people room, but not licence to abuse the genuine liberty a Christian community should enjoy. For instance, why would I give to an unknown visitor during a main Sunday service, the freedom to bring what he said was "a word from God", when he point blank refused to share with me the main thought of his "word"? Liberty, in this context, does not mean a "free for all" opportunity to speak.

On the other hand, why would I stop known, godly, praying people from bringing words of encouragement to the body of Christ or deny the opportunity for those with emerging gifts to preach and develop in major gatherings? I remind myself that others gave me an opportunity to speak when I wasn't very good and I am still a learner!

When a group of elders take seriously the responsibility to guide, govern, guard and gather any Christian community, I believe they provide a safe secure environment – like a godly father in a family home – for all around them to grow and flourish.

A commitment to heed the injunction of Christ to go and preach the gospel and make disciples with a purposeful commitment to seeing Christ formed in others, draws the promise of Jesus to "build His church" into a sharp, personal and dynamic focus, as each of us living stones become carriers of God and together we are a "habitation" – a dwelling in which God lives by His Spirit (Ephesians 2:22). That is the Church – the presence-carrying community that reveals Jesus to a tired and hungry world, offers light in darkness and hope in despair. I am honoured and thrilled to be a part of it (warts and all!). It is the "thing" Jesus loves, "for He loves the church" (Ephesians 5:25)

I think I understand the rationale and reserve of those who have become sceptical of organised religion, including many dynamic evangelical and charismatic groups with significant organisation and structure. They fear the loss of the "organic", the dynamic, the flexible and unique expression of a Christian community that the New Testament seems to model.

We have a human tendency to institutionalise once vital organisations. The care of the sick became over-elaborate, bureaucratic, monolithic. The teaching of the young, stuffy, inflexible, and impersonal. Any church carries the same risk. In larger congregations the leaders, the staff, the organisation and its administration can become the centre that the people, its congregation, come to serve and support. The programmes and priorities of "the organisation" end up squeezing out and marginalising dynamic life and spontaneity.

If we understand a presence-carrying, discipling model of church, however, what has been seen as the centre, the core, the structure, becomes merely the "wrapper" around the new centre and core, which is the people. Then the work of the leaders and staff is centred on helping them all to find their true place and become all that they were created to be – in other words, presence carrying, growing disciples. This provides empowerment and enables the flexible and unique expressions of Christian community that God wants to use to impact and change this world in which we live.

I pray that each of us has the opportunity to experience a sense of awe and wonder in worship. That the songs we sing are much more about Him than "I", "me" or "us". That when the Bible is opened we receive inspiration and revelation and that the truth sets us free. That in our times of meeting and worship we are drawn towards the Lord and not driven by human agencies. That we all learn how to be fully present when God's presence intensifies, and that we carry an expectancy that "God will be God" – that miraculous things may happen and we will be transformed in His company. May the Welcome, the Word and the Worship all be "sweet smelling offerings to God". All this will help us nurture a presence-carrying culture.

I said at the beginning of this chapter that we would also look at some issues around the question, "What can only I do to nurture His presence?" We will deal with some negatives first.

Jesus makes it abundantly clear in teaching His disciples to pray, that unforgiveness is a massive stumbling block to spiritual growth and consciously knowing the presence of God. We looked at this in greater detail in an earlier chapter. What about bitterness and past pain? I was reading in *Begin the Journey with the Daily Office* this morning a reflection about Joseph from Genesis 45:

"He did not minimise or rationalise the painful years. Joseph could have destroyed his brothers in anger. But out of the honest grieving of his pain he truly forgave and was able to bless the brothers who had betrayed him ... How did he do it? Joseph had clearly developed a secret history over a long period of time in his relationship with God. His whole life was structured around following the Lord God of Israel. Then when the moment came for a critical decision, he was ready."[17]

The daily reflection then asked a question: "What pains in your life are waiting to be acknowledged and grieved? It then finished with a challenging but helpful prayer:

"Lord, forgive me of my sins as I forgive those who have hurt me. Lead me through the process of grieving and healing that I might offer genuine kindness to those who have not been kind to me. Help me, like Joseph, to join with you to become a blessing to many other people. In Jesus' name, Amen."

Now let us think about the company we keep. In 1 Corinthians 15:33 Paul says, *"Bad company corrupts good character."* Company here includes both people and conversations. What do the people you are with talk about? Do they draw you towards or away from a desire for more of the presence of God? Each of us must answer for ourselves. Each of us must deal with life's negatives. Deal with them now or as soon as is practical. It is not my purpose to cover an all-embracing list of negatives, only to highlight and illustrate the principle and leave the details for the Holy Spirit to prompt each of us about whatever it is He wants us to recognise and change.

If bad company has a negative effect, then good company and conversation, by the same token, will have a positive impact.

So we should make sure that we have positive stimuli flowing into our lives and be very attentive about what our "eye gate", "thought gate" and "emotions gate" allow into our lives. There are huge influences in and around our modern lives that distract, deflect and unhelpfully occupy our time and attention. The Bible encourages us to be "on our guard". Make sure that "good conversation" is stimulating your everyday enjoyment of the presence of God.

There is a business statement that says, "Where trust is high and cost is low, speed is fast."[18]

Obviously, the opposite is also true. When trust is low and cost is high, speed is slow. The Bible says we should, *"trust in the Lord with all* [our] *heart ... and He will direct* [our] *paths."* So when trust in God is high, cost is low, and we make significant progress. What does this trust look like? Here is a starter to stimulate your thinking:

T – truth. There is no trust without truth

R – reliability and relationship. I once heard a preacher say, "You can't drive 10-tonne trucks over plywood bridges."

U – unity. How can we walk together unless we agree? He, God, is not about to change, so who must?

S – sensitivity. Another Bible and Steven Covey truth: seek first to understand

T – time. Developing trust takes time

Don't compromise here. It costs too much, including more wasted time!

What other action words, like Trust, do you need to invest in, to help you nurture a culture that is welcoming of God's presence? Could Faith, Hope and Love be worth developing?

I mentioned earlier the amazing level of dependence Jesus had on His Father – *"By myself, I can do nothing."* Is there a clue here from Jesus for us? If and when we practice a conscious dependence on God we will be cultivating and nurturing a life where we cannot live, and stop trying to live, without the presence of God. For instance, we will pray differently if we are aware of "Emmanuel", God being with us. It will be more a conversation than a monologue and it will grow to become more listening than speaking. What He says is more important than any contribution I make to the dialogue!

I will finish this chapter with two dangerous words: *discipline* and *addiction*. Reading 1 Corinthians 9 again recently, I was reminded of the strong and demanding language Paul uses. He uses the illustration of the Olympic athlete who invests a huge amount of effort to win a prize "that will not last". Then he produces one of his oft-used words: "therefore".

"Therefore, I do not run like a man running aimlessly; I do not fight like a man beating the air. No, I beat my body and make it my slave so that after I have preached to others, I myself will not be disqualified for the prize." (1 Corinthians 9:24-27)

Maybe in a world of quick fix "almost everything" and easy option living, we would be wise to capture Paul's commitment, including an urgency and intensity in our pursuit of the presence of God.

Finally, *addiction*. It is always very traumatic to see someone trapped in substance addiction, when their craving drives them to extreme lengths. But reverse the negative. How strong is our desire to know God, to be in His company, to be unable to fully live without Him? The thought provides quite a challenge. Did the poems of the old hymn writers glimpse this level of dependency and desire? An addiction to the presence of God? Here are the opening lines of three hymns on a page open in front of me:

> "Nearer, still nearer, close to thy heart, draw me, my Saviour, so precious thou art."

> "If I but knew thee as thou art, O loveliness unknown."

> "I cannot breathe enough of thee, O gentle breeze of love."

Were they addicted? Probably!

So what must remain and what must change in my life so that I more powerfully encounter God and nurture a presence-carrying culture? What needs to happen in my wider world that will make a positive impact on the culture I live in, so that it welcomes God more? If Paul had to attend to his possible disqualification, then you and I must answer these important questions too.

I remember standing, singing next to my mother as a young boy. One particular short hymn floods my heart and mind. It was sung to an almost plainsong tune. I leave you with its words...

Jesus, stand among us
In thy risen power
Let this time of worship
Be a hallowed hour

Breathe thy Holy Spirit
Into every heart
Bid the fears and sorrows
From each soul depart

Thus with quickened footsteps
We'll pursue our way
Watching for the dawning
Of eternal day

10
Revering His Presence

Author Mark Tabb writes,

"The Bible begins with a very simple statement: 'In the beginning God created the heavens and the earth.' Everything that follows builds on this one statement. If the first verse of the Bible isn't true, the rest of it is irrelevant and so are our lives. The reason is simple: If God did not create the heavens and the earth, if the physical universe is all there is and all there ever will be, then every possible source of meaning and happiness is just as temporary and arbitrary as the universe itself. All are nothing more than futile attempts to make ourselves feel better. If the universe just happened, it doesn't mean anything, and neither do we.

However, if God indeed created the heavens and the earth, the physical universe ceases to be our only frame of reference.

The presence of the image of God within us is why we long for something we cannot find in the world in which we live. When God made us like Himself, He placed in us a longing for the eternal – that which is permanent – deep within our souls."[19]

Something in every human longs for a connection with the Eternal Creator; an uncaused, uncreated and unaccountable God. People ignore it, suppress it, divert it, substitute lesser "gods" for it, but I believe the wise agree with Ecclesiastes. The writer states that there is a time for everything and illustrates his point with a long list including a time to be born, a time to be silent and a time to love. Later he writes, *"He has also set eternity in the hearts of men, yet they cannot fathom what God has done from beginning to end."* He says that men should be happy and do good while they live and everyone should eat and drink and find satisfaction in their work. All this is a gift from God.

Then he declares that everything God does will last forever, nothing added or taken away. God does all this, *"So that men will revere Him."* God is reaching into our temporary, time-limited world with a commitment to our temporal blessing, but with a deeper longing that we would reconnect with His eternal reality by learning, loving and living with reverence for Him.

If, as I truly believe, this is true, then the hideous separation of the sacred and the secular is ludicrous. There is no separation – all can be holy, everything enjoyed and God be always present and honoured. So the first principle of revering His presence is a *commitment to live a holistic life* – God involved and welcomed into every part of it, no separation between who I am and how I act at home, at work, in church, everywhere and anywhere. The Jewish community thank God for the ordinary and the divine, from the vastness of the universe to the blessing of correctly functioning "human plumbing"; from a table with food to a holy festival, from making money to almsgiving. God is involved in anything and everything.

From this understanding it is an easy step to the second principle: *the whole of life is an act of worship to God.* Paul, in his amazing Romans treatise, summarises this with another of his "therefores": *"Therefore, I urge you, brothers, in view of God's mercy, to offer your bodies as living sacrifices, holy and pleasing to God, this is your spiritual act of worship"* (Romans 12:1). He calls for a transformation of mind, breaking from conformity to "the pattern of this world" and promises that in so living we can know and enjoy God's perfect will. As Jesus, we will live dependent on God, listening for direction, living to please our Father in heaven. The whole of life becomes an offering that brings God's smile and pleases Him.

In the language of the Hebrew Shema in Deuteronomy 6:4-9, the faithful make a daily confession which includes, *"Love the Lord your God with all your heart and with all your soul and with all your strength."* Then, speaking about God's gift of commandments, he writes, *"Impress them on your children. Talk about them when you sit at home and when you walk along the road, when you lie down and when you get up..."* All of life is represented in this full confession.

What does that look like today, yes literally today, as I write? I woke this morning thanking God for His goodness, had something light to eat, and caught up with the news developments in a changing world. I spent an hour plus reading the Bible and in the quietness enjoyed being with God.

Then followed a little ritual of preparing breakfast for my wife of forty-six years and attending to some chores. Dorothy is leaving to visit her aging, ailing mum, and I am sitting at my desk writing, praying and believing that you will capture the "act of worship" that my words are to God. Builders are currently working in my house, but thankfully not today! My youngest grandson may want to ride the lawn mower with Poppa later. My son and his family are overseas. I pray they will enjoy rest and recreation and be daily conscious of God's loving presence. Today has no formal church leadership activity, no preaching, no so-called "spiritual work", but everything is my worship to God; being the best man I can be in all the areas of my life and remembering that in my flawed, frailty, I am forgiven, loved and accepted. Lord, help me live to please you today.

Eugene Petersen in his excellent book, *Under the Unpredictable Plant*, speaks about the rule and disciplines that have developed through the centuries of Christian community. He summarises the rule as, "Daily praying the Psalms surrounded by Lord's Day worship with your community and recollected prayer through the hours of the day."

We would be wise, whatever our history and spiritual tradition, to learn from many godly men and women who have preceded us. They learned how to focus a life of worship, weaving the divine and mundane into every warp and woof of life. Petersen then amplifies the rule with the fourteen most accepted spiritual disciplines:

- spiritual reading
- spiritual direction
- meditation
- confession
- bodily exercise
- fasting
- Sabbath-keeping
- dream interpretation
- retreats
- pilgrimage
- almsgiving (including tithing)
- journaling
- sabbaticals
- small groups

Each of us, at each stage of our life, needs to find the rhythm that helps us live all of life as worship to God.

If we understand these principles and are serious about living them out in reverence to and for God, it will become obvious, but no less important, to state that we will learn to acknowledge the Lord in everything and live with deep thankfulness to God, expressed in simple acts of service for Him and others, with a conscious gratitude for all the blessings we receive.

Let us now think about another principle: *the need to develop our spiritual hunger.* Heidi Baker, who with her husband Rolland leads the amazing IRIS Ministries in Mozambique and neighbouring nations, contends that, "The hungriest people always get fed." This was her reflection on the desperate plight of the poor, starving people they regularly feed on the rubbish dumps of Maputo – but with an added spiritual implication. So, how hungry are we?

The world around us is constantly seeking to entice us into an addictive slavery to our natural appetites and desires. Our consumerist world makes an economic virtue out of spending, whether we need what we buy or not. Maybe for us, the secret is to nurture a different hunger. What might help such a pursuit?

First, we should move from a "getting" to a "giving" mindset. Our starting point ceases to be, "What's in it for me?" to one where we consciously look to be a blessing to others. A friend told me a story last week. After preaching about Moses taking off his sandals when he encountered God (recorded in Exodus 3:5), he urged his congregation to leave their shoes at the end of the service as an act of worship and to help the many poor people they were clothing in their inner-city community. Five hundred pairs of shoes were left in church that day.

Second, we should fill ourselves with God rather than other things. Many people forget that we are always full of something. The Bible says that, *out of the overflow of the heart, the mouth speaks* (Matthew 12:34). Let us therefore make sure that we are full of good things. Then, when life gives us a knock, as it does in whatever way it chooses, what spills out of us is godly and good.

Third, we should live more intentionally and be less careless and indifferent about how we use our time, talent and treasure and more focused on "abiding" in Him. We realise that without "root" there is no "fruit"; that if we fail to resource our lives by "abiding in the vine" we soon become ineffective and much less productive. We will never drift into a focused and fruitful life. We need to be intentional, feed the right hunger, cut off the unproductive branches and learn a greater dependence on God.

Thinking further about how we encourage a life of revering God's presence, I am drawn to reflect on the principle and power of blessing. The Old Testament Aaronic priesthood were given a responsibility to bless the people. They were instructed to speak over them these words:

"The Lord bless you and keep you; the Lord make His face shine upon you and be gracious to you; the Lord turn His face toward you and give you peace." (Numbers 6:24-26)

The instruction finishes, *"So they will put my name on the Israelites, and I will bless them."* How do we "put His name on" the people around us? How do we give and receive a blessing? I am exercised about this both in speaking a "blessing" in more formal, gathered contexts, whether church services or rite-of-passage events like weddings, births, dedications and funerals. But also in the informal sharing of life in conversation, food and fun.

I have said many times, I am not sure how this "blessing thing" works, but I know that it does. It is a pain to me that on so many occasions we miss the moment. We have worshipped God and the service will end with an announcement about coffee (nothing wrong with coffee!), but no spoken blessing. Or at a meal table with family or friends the moment is missed to bless and encourage.

Years ago I was helped in my understanding whilst on a ministry trip to Central America. I was with a large congregation in Guatemala City with a lovely man of God, Harold Caballeros. At the end of a great service that I had the privilege of preaching in, Harold spoke a blessing over the thousands gathered in the big tent they worshiped in at that time. He spoke God's commanded favour and blessing, identifying many specific areas of life. It was electrifying. He had learned how to speak the blessing and the congregation had learned how to receive it. I have sought to develop my ability to speak God's blessing and to teach people how to receive it. If we revere God we will understand that His *makarios* – His blessing – is the overflow of His heart and longing to bless us, His people.

Reflecting on the Numbers 6 blessing again, we see that it speaks of His face shining on us and of His turning His face towards us. Think about that for a moment. Who can remember when Mum or Dad or some authority figure like a school teacher used to say, "Look at me when I'm talking to you!" Remember that? More than an issue of politeness and good behaviour, it was about attention, being fully present, being focused on what was said.

I think God would say the same to us – not out of chastisement, but for connection and attention. He turns His face towards us because He wants us to receive something that only He can give us, His *makarios*, His blessing! So, learn to receive from Him and then pass His blessing on to others.

I had a unique experience of this again recently. I was in quiet prayer in my study at home early one morning when I had a sudden gush of words about a number of specific issues around my life and ministry. I heard myself speak very directly to God. I was very clear about timing and the "when", "what" and "why" in this unusual prayer. A short time later, I was involved in a leaders' conference in Addis Ababa, Ethiopia. Late on the first day of the conference I found myself at the back of the room as the afternoon session was finishing. The national leader of the group of churches was praying a blessing and all those in the room lifted their arms and held their hands forward. Something spiritual and powerful was happening, even though I did not understand exactly what, because of the lack of language interpretation. But, I felt the Lord say to me, "You are to ask for that blessing before you leave the conference on Thursday evening."

The conference continued for two days. Then it was time for the session to end and for me to leave for the airport and it had been a joy to be involved. I asked the brothers and sisters to give me a blessing. I was invited to kneel down, only confirming what I felt the Holy Spirit had instructed me to do. The leaders gathered round. Some laid hands on me, the whole group raised their hands towards me and they prayed. I felt the same gush of words I had spoken in my study, those weeks before, but this time I was receiving the blessing as the answer, the fulfilment, the provision in a specific time frame, of all these things that I had placed before the Lord.

I now wait with expectation for His miraculous intervention. The answers require miracles and I am encouraged that some of the specific things are already changing in our favour. I believe in God's blessing. As I revere His name I more fully understand His commitment to bless. It is my responsibility to learn how to "look at Him" and receive what He wants to give me.

Part of the act of reverence is to defer and be attentive. It involves more listening than speaking, understanding our place without fear. Yes, we are welcome at the Father's table, but we also know who He is – Almighty God.

What I write about next has been known and practiced by some traditions for a very long time. Learning to be still, finding inner solitude and practicing silence are disciplines that were rarely spoken about in my Pentecostal youth, not visibly practiced by many or seen by the majority as important in the development of a reverential walk with God.

Looking back, I am glad for many things in my spiritual formation, but sad that these issues were untaught or exampled. Wherever you are on a personal journey to a deeper, richer, inner life, refuse to be discouraged. Hold with passion whatever biblical base represents your spirituality and come with openness and vulnerability to the unknown parts of a spiritual discipline that may call you to discover God in new ways.

Let us think about inner solitude first. I found this quote from Henri Nouwen very demanding:

"Solitude is the furnace of transformation. Without solitude we remain victims of our society and continue to be entangled in the illusions of the false self. Jesus Himself entered this furnace and there He was tempted with the three compulsions of the world: to be relevant ("turn stones into loaves"), to be spectacular ("throw yourself down"), and to be powerful ("I will give you all these kingdoms"). There He affirmed God as the only source of His identity ("You must worship the Lord your God and serve Him alone"). Solitude is the place of the great struggle and the great encounter – the struggle against the compulsions of the false self, and the encounter with the loving God who offers Himself as the substance of the new self. In solitude I get rid of my scaffolding: no friends to talk with, no telephone calls to make … The task is to persevere in my solitude, to stay in my cell until all my seductive visitors get tired of pounding on my door and leave me alone."[20]

I have tasted something of this "getting rid of my scaffolding", this "struggle with the false self", but I am not in any way accomplished in this discipline. It beckons me forward as it did the Desert Fathers and many others over the generations. Part of my journey is the practice of the presence of God, finding a place of shalom (peace) in the midst of busyness and noise. Recognising the need to limit the spiritual and emotional "caffeine agents" that provoke fear and frenzy, play on insecurities and unhealthy doubt, and cripple our inner life with distraction and a preoccupation with the less important. But, hey, I'm a self confessed beginner!

For an activist, and I'm one of that kind, an inner solitude that helps me be still is a spiritual journey. I accept that part of my experience may be to do with the passing of the years, but the biblical injunction is much more urgent than that.

"Be still and know that I am God" (Psalm 46:10) carries several connotations:

Be weak – you cannot do it in your own strength. "When I am weak, then I am strong."

Stop work – let God accomplish what only God can do. Rest in Him.

Start relying – actively trust, lean on God and His promises. Ceasing from self-effort and striving is much more than inactivity or passivity. It expresses a profound belief and reverence for God through faith and trust.

What about the value of silence, learning how to turn off the noise of life, the demands of a to-do list, the expectations of others, and silencing every other voice apart from His? We will be helped if we first turn off and tune out all actual noise in our time of silence, and then the superficial "inner voice" that demands our attention. Then we can begin to enjoy an inner silence that knows many levels, into which comes His voice – through Scripture, thoughts, ideas, promptings, pictures and much more.

I was privileged to attend the Leadership Summit at Willow Creek, Chicago recently. One of a galaxy of great speakers was a Coptic Christian who is known as Mama Maggie (often called the Mother Theresa of Cairo). She has devoted her life to the needs of the poorest of the poor in Cairo's ghettos and developed a deep spirituality. She is long practiced in the discipline of silence and summarised her journey in these phrases:

• Silence your body to listen to your words

• Silence your words to listen to your thoughts

• Silence your thoughts to listen to your heart

- Silence your heart to listen to your spirit

- Silence your spirit to listen to His Spirit

She urged her listeners, "to leave the many and our self for the one." She expresses my own desire in better words than mine and I pray you will find them as compelling as I did and still do.

The final stop in this chapter, reflecting on revering His presence, brings me to the principle of "allowing" God to be God.

Please immediately understand that, of course, we can never prevent God from being God. He has always been God, is God and always will be God – the unerring and unchanging God of all gods. By "allowing" I mean in the limiting sense, where we cease to interfere in things bigger than us, stop meddling in God's business, being and doing only that which is our responsibility and leaving the rest in His hands.

I remember hearing a classical violin soloist playing in a magnificent concert hall on one occasion. The sound was wonderful. The violin only played that way because of its construction, the maestro's skill and the appropriate tension on the strings. Similarly, God has created us to be carriers of His life. He knows what will help us make the best sound. We don't always like it, but that does include having the right level of *tension* in our lives. Naturally and spiritually there are issues that cannot be easily sorted out. As Andy Stanley once said regarding many of the challenges of life that we face, "They are not problems that can be solved, but tensions that have to be managed." Not every difficulty in life can be resolved.

In the area of Christian doctrine, there are apparent opposites that must be held in tension in our understanding, for both are true. In the normal flow of life, why do some die too young and others seem to live too long? Why do some have more than enough and many not enough? How can living a life, believing in excellence, and doing things well and to the best of our ability, be reconciled with a budget and finite resources? How do we find the balance between our lives being under-challenged, so that we are left unfulfilled and under-achieving, and over-challenged, so that we are stretched too far, producing unhealthy levels of stress and the possibility of potential break down?

Paul invites us to, *"Make it your ambition to lead a quiet life, to mind your own business and to work with your hands, just as we told you"* (1 Thessalonians 4:11). In other words, let God be God, trust Him, do only His "commanded" work, don't interfere with things that are too big for us – including holding onto the steering wheel of our lives.

All this means I must come to live with many paradoxes. As I have written before, it is not so much an "either/or" question but an "and" answer. This means that I must reverence God. Many things are bigger than me, but they are most certainly not bigger than Him. He knows everything. I can trust that He will do all things well – even the parts I don't understand or even think are wrong!

I remember as a teenager, that Saturday night was often a fellowship evening in the church my father led. People would tend to sing a solo, give a testimony, briefly speak about a Bible text or sometimes ask a question. The questions were often around eschatological beliefs to do with the second coming of Jesus – a hot topic.

My mother and father had some different views on that! There was often strong disagreement and sometimes the meeting ended on less than the most harmonious note.

How sad, especially when Paul teaches about the coming of the Lord that in any conversation we *"...should encourage each other with these words"* (1 Thessalonians 4:18).

I made the decision, half a century ago, that I would never be in the position of allowing things that should "encourage us" to divide us, simply because we don't have a complete knowledge or understanding of them. God knows, the time is in His hands, He will work everything out. So let's trust Him. He does know best.

The Pentecostal in me, after being still and silent, now wants to say "Hallelujah!"

Conclusion

And now to a brief conclusion. While this book has come to its final stages before printing, the building work on my home has ended, the disruption is over and we are enjoying some new space, including this lovely study I am sitting in. Following a breathtaking sunset and a lovely dinner with Dorothy Ann, I am enjoying the stillness and better ordered space in which to work and write these words.

However, to get to this position, I can still remember big holes in the ground, burst pipes, pumped concrete and all the expected ingredients of a building programme, and yes, some unexpected moments too.

Maybe this reality is also a parable. We enjoyed our home before, but today is better than yesterday. Yes, I have enjoyed my developing understanding of being a Presence Carrier, the many sublime experiences and encounters with God that have shaped my life and ministry. However, there is a thirst for more and I have this feeling that what happened in the building work is happening spiritually. To sit in a new place with God may need some change, disruption, inconvenience, cost and even temporary chaos. It was worth it naturally, it must be worth it spiritually too.

I pray that your reading of this book has at least provoked you to plan to be in a better place. It may have been part of the building work to help you realise your plan. If so, sorry for the cost and chaos, mess and disruption I have caused you! But it is worth it.

We were created in God's image and likeness and the more of His presence we carry, the better that image and likeness will be seen. We were re-created in Christ to make that a dynamic possibility. The more like Him we become, the more His presence in us will change our world and help us fulfil His purpose and hear His "well done."

Charles Swindoll tells a story about an animal school where the ducks were great at swimming but very poor runners. In trying to make them better runners their teachers made them worse swimmers. Let each of us be the person we were uniquely created to be, use our gifts to the full, and represent Jesus in a broken, hope-starved world.

Our story may be found on a page in the London Times like Surgeon Vice Admiral Sir James Watt: "...a committed Christian throughout his long and active life, founder member of Naval Christian Fellowship" or we may die apparently forgotten. God has unveiled in each of us gifts and a plan that needs to be outworked. A better account than the London Times is being written in another place. Let us make sure that, with God's help and presence, all that should be written about us is in that book. Our lives will be richer and more fulfilling, the world will be a better place, many will thank God that you lived or they met you, God's kingdom will come and He will be glorified.

So what will you do to help bring this to reality? What must change? What must end or begin?

Francis of Assisi reported that Christ spoke to him, "Francis, go and repair my house. You see it is falling down."

If these words apply to the building of your "house", please hear His voice. God waits with expectation.

Will we be newly attentive?!

End notes

1. Lucado, Max, *Travelling Light* (Thomas Nelson, 2009), pp55-56.

2. Ibid. p57

3. Ibid. pp58-59

4. Scazerro, Peter, *Begin The Journey With the Daily Office* (self-published, further details available from the author's website: http://www.emotionallyhealthy.org), p88.

5. Tozer, A.W., Leaning Into The Wind (Creation House, 1983).

6. Garner, Albert, *Highlights From An Adventure of Faith* (self-published), p52.

7. Daily Office p26, 166 from Gilliam R Evans' translation and foreword of Bernard of Clairvaux: Selected works, Classics of Western Spirituality (1987).

8. Scazzero, Peter, *Daily Office*, p2.

9. *Kezazah* – If a Jewish boy in first century Paliestine wasted his family inheritance among Gentiles and then dared to return home, the village performed what is called the Kezazah ceremony. In this ceremony, the village breaks a large pot in front of the boy, symbolically portraying and officially proclaiming the separation between the boy and the village. (Bailey, Kenneth, *Jesus Through Middle Eastern Eyes: Cultural Studies in the Gospels*, SPCK, 2008).

10. Bailey, Kenneth, *The Cross and the Prodigal* (InterVarsity Press, 2005).

11. Jamison, Abbot Christopher, *Finding Sanctuary* (Phoenix, 2007), p84.

12. Ibid. p84.

13. Ibid. p85.

14. Ibid. pp85-86

15. Scazzero, Peter, *Daily Office*

16. White, Canon Andrew, *Faith Under Fire* (Monarch 2011), p105.

17. Scazzero, Peter, *Daily Office,* pp49-50.

18. Covey, Steven M., *The Speed of Trust* (Simon & Schuster, 2006)

19. Tabb, Mark, *Living With Less*, Broadman and Holman Publishers, 2006), pp8-90.

20. Nouwen, Henri, *The Daily Office*, p29.

21. Published obituary.